Vocabulary Development

It all begins with words. Whether you're reading, writing, or talking, you're using words. Even when you're thinking—even when you're dreaming!—you do it mainly in words.

It makes sense, then, to learn as many words as you can.

You already know a lot of words. There are many that you use in conversation, but many more that you can understand when you read them. This unit is all about vocabulary development—learning the meanings of new words and how to use them.

- **In Lesson 1,** you'll learn about context clues—how to figure out the meanings of new words when you read them by relating them to words in the sentence or paragraph that you already know. You'll learn how to tell which meaning of a word is meant in the case of words that can have more than one meaning. You'll add new words to your vocabulary by adding parts to words you know.

- **Lesson 2** is all about words that don't mean exactly what they say. You'll learn how to recognize figurative language—words that writers use to let you perceive things in new and different ways, especially in poetry. You'll learn about idioms, adages, and proverbs—phrases that mean something quite different from the individual words in them. And you'll learn how to distinguish among the meanings of words that mean *almost* the same thing, and between quite different words that happen to be spelled the same way.

- **Lesson 3** is about those words that you may not use in conversation or encounter regularly in your reading, but that are important to know when you're reading about specific topics. You'll learn how to use context clues to discover the meanings of those special terms used in science, social studies, and other subjects.

Now turn the page and start building your vocabulary!

Word Meanings

L.5.4, RL.5.4, RI.5.4

When you were very young, you learned all your words by listening. Sometimes you may have asked an adult "What's that?" and were told, "That's a car," or "That's a tree." But mostly you learned new words by hearing people use them. You learned from adults, from other children, even from TV and songs. You figured out what words mean by the way they related to the words you already know. You learned new words by using **context clues.**

Now you can read. You can probably read a lot more words than you use in conversation. But even if you run into a word you don't know, you can often figure out its meaning by **context clues** in the sentence or paragraph.

Context Clues

Read these sentences from *M. C. Higgins the Great,* by Virginia Hamilton.

> Mayo Cornelius Higgins raised his arms high to the sky and spread them wide. He glanced furtively around. It was all right. There was no one to see him greeting the coming sunrise.

Do you know what the word *furtively* means? If you don't, you can figure out its meaning from the words and ideas around them. You have two context clues. First, because it ends in *-ly,* you know it's an adverb, describing the way Mayo looked around. The second clue is in the sentences before and after. Why did he look around? Because he didn't want anyone to see him greeting the sunrise. You know enough about people's feelings to guess that he might have been embarrassed. You can guess that *furtively* means "in a way so as not to be noticed," or *secretly.*

Context clues may come in several forms:

Context Clues

Synonyms	Words that have nearly the same meanings
Examples	Words that show what another word means
Definitions	Words that tell what another word means
Descriptions	Words that tell you more about a word, such as by comparison or by explaining an action it causes

Synonyms

You might find a word in the sentence or paragraph that means nearly the same thing as another word. If you know one word, you can figure out the other.

> We expected a village of rude <u>dwellings</u> and were surprised to find neat, modern houses instead.

The words *houses* and *dwellings* both name buildings where people live. Even if you didn't know the meaning of <u>dwellings</u>, you could figure out from the context that it means basically the same as *houses*.

Examples

In other paragraphs, you can figure out the meaning of an unknown word by examples that point to what it means.

> He spoke with Julie, who was a paleontologist from the university. She told him the best places to look for fossils after he promised not to take any home as souvenirs.

What does <u>paleontologist</u> mean? The context shows that it's a noun, and the *-ologist* ending suggests that it's a kind of scientist. But the example shows that Julie knows about fossils. You can figure out that <u>paleontologist</u> means "a scientist who studies prehistoric life."

Definitions

Sometimes a word is directly defined in context. Look for definitions in these sentences:

> He was a compelling speaker who held the audience's attention, but what he said was all moonshine. When you thought about it, nothing he said made any sense.

<u>Compelling</u> is a word that you may not read or hear very often, and <u>moonshine</u> may suggest only something you see on a clear night. But the paragraphs give you definitions. The context tells you that <u>compelling</u> means "holding one's attention," and <u>moonshine</u> means "empty, foolish talk."

Descriptions

Sometimes a sentence will contain a description to tell you what a word means. The description might be a *comparison* with something you know. Or, it might show you a *relationship* between the new word and the one you know.

> Bears may look like slow, lumbering animals, but they can move with alacrity when they feel threatened.

You may not know the word <u>alacrity</u>, but you can tell by comparison with *slow* and *lumbering* that it means "speed."

> A cat in England called Oscar lost his rear paws in a terrible accident with a farm machine. But veterinarians fitted him with a pair of prosthetic paws.

The word <u>prosthetic</u> may be new to you, too. But Oscar had to be fitted with paws because he lost his own. You can figure out that <u>prosthetic</u> means "artificial but lifelike."

Guided Practice

July 21, 1761—We have reached the Miami villages. Chief Heart-of-Oak prepared a feast for us. Swift-as-a-Deer was true to his word. His people are most <u>hospitable</u> to guests. I am <u>fortunate</u> that he has educated me as to the ways of the Miamis. To honor his guests, the chief placed food directly into our mouths, as one feeds an <u>infant</u>. This is not an agreeable custom to Englishmen. Had I not been advised of it, I might have offended my hosts by showing my <u>revulsion</u>.

Make sure you know the exact meaning of the new words in this passage by checking their meaning in a print or online dictionary.

The word <u>hospitable</u> means _____.

- **A** ill
- **B** warlike
- **C** proud and strong
- **D** kind and welcoming

When you read the paragraph, you can find an example that tells you what <u>hospitable</u> means. The clue is that the Miamis gave their visitors a feast. That clue doesn't fit ill, warlike, or proud and strong, but if you substitute "kind and welcoming," you see that the correct answer is choice D.

The word <u>fortunate</u> means _____.

- **A** rich
- **B** lucky
- **C** amused
- **D** embarrassed

To answer this question, you need to consider the entire paragraph. The English visitor is glad that Swift-as-a-Deer has taught him his people's customs because it kept him from insulting them. That wouldn't make the visitor feel rich, amused, or embarrassed, but it would make him feel "lucky." Choice B is the correct answer.

An <u>infant</u> means the same as _____.

    A   a pet

    B   a baby

    C   an enemy

    D   an honored guest

> ✓ Understanding this word involves making a comparison in your mind. Would you feed a pet, an enemy, or an honored guest by placing food directly into its mouth? The correct answer is choice B.

<u>Revulsion</u> is a word that means _____.

    A   fear

    B   disgust

    C   curiosity

    D   confusion

Explain your answer to the last question.

_____

_____

> ✓ Choice B is the correct answer to the multiple-choice question. Here is a sample answer for the question above:

If someone surprised me by putting food in my mouth, I wouldn't be afraid, curious, or confused, but I would certainly be disgusted!

Words With Multiple Meanings

Some words have more than one meaning. A dictionary will list each meaning separately, usually with a number in front. The different meanings may be spelled and even pronounced alike. But if you don't know all the meanings, you may not understand what you're reading. Here are some of the many meanings of the word press:

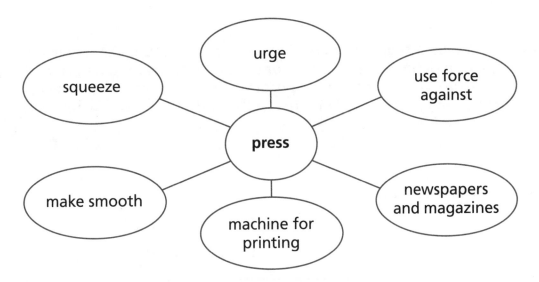

When you come across a word like press in a sentence, you can use context clues to find out its meaning. First, notice how it is used in the sentence. What part of speech is it? Is it a verb (action word), a noun (the name of a person, place, or thing), or an adjective (a word that describes)?

> Whenever I visit my aunt and uncle, they press me to stay longer.

In this sentence, you can tell that press is a verb. Which of the meanings shown above are verbs? There are four of them. Substitute each meaning for the word press in the sentence. The one that makes the most sense is "urge."

Guided Practice

Read the passage. Then answer the questions.

The message was in cipher. Someone had used a knife with a keen blade to carve it. Cora knew that the others were waiting at the coast. There would be food there, and a warm campfire. But what if the message was for her, from Jason? She had to take a few minutes to puzzle it out.

Check the exact meaning of the new words in this passage by checking their meaning in a print or online dictionary.

The word <u>cipher</u> in this passage means ____.

  A to do arithmetic

  B the number zero

  C code or secret writing

  D an unimportant person

> ✓ As used in the passage, the word <u>cipher</u> is plainly a noun. That eliminates choice A, which defines a verb. Which of the other choices could have to do with a message? "Zero" or "an unimportant person" don't make sense in this context. The phrase "puzzle it out" at the end of the passage tells you that the answer is choice C.

What is meant by <u>keen</u> in this passage?

  A sharp   **C** desirable, "cool"

  B eager   **D** to weep and wail

> ✓ <u>Keen</u> may have any of these meanings. But the context tells you that it is an adjective here, so choice D can't be correct. Can a knife blade be "eager"? Do you associate "cool" with carving a message on wood? You can figure out that choice A is the correct answer.

What does the word <u>coast</u> mean in this passage? Explain your answer.

_____

_____

_____

_____

> ✓ Here is a sample answer:

It means "seashore." In this passage, <u>coast</u> is used as a noun. It could mean either "seashore" or "a ride down a hill, powered by gravity," as on a roller coaster, but it doesn't sound as if Cora is on her way to an amusement park.

UNIT 1 ▨▨▨▨▨▨▨▨▨▨▨▨▨▨▨▨▨▨▨▨▨▨▨▨▨▨▨▨▨▨▨▨▨▨▨▨▨▨
Vocabulary Development

Using Prefixes, Suffixes, and Root Words _____

You often can learn new words because you already understand parts of them. A **prefix** is a part of a word added to the beginning of the word that changes the meaning of the word. If you know the word <u>agree</u>, and you know that the prefix *dis-* means "not," you can figure out that <u>disagree</u> means "not agree."

A **suffix** is a part added to the end of a word that changes the meaning of the word. If you know the word <u>fear</u>, and you know that the suffix *-less* means "without," you can figure out that <u>fearless</u> means "without fear."

Most prefixes and suffixes come from Latin and Greek words. For example, the prefix *tri-* comes from the Latin word for "three." Think of words like *triangle* and *tricycle*.

Some Common Prefixes

Prefix	Meaning	Example
bi-	two	<u>bi</u>cycle
dis-	not	<u>dis</u>agree
ex-	out, away from	<u>ex</u>tinct
extra-	beyond	<u>extra</u>terrestrial
in-	in or not	<u>in</u>expensive
mis-	bad or not	<u>mis</u>behave
multi-	many	<u>multi</u>colored
non-	not	<u>non</u>sense
pre-	before	<u>pre</u>view
re-	back, again	<u>re</u>play
sub-	under, less than	<u>sub</u>divide
trans-	through, over, across	<u>trans</u>continental
un-	not	<u>un</u>pleasant
uni-	one	<u>uni</u>form

Some Common Suffixes

Suffix	Meaning	Example
-able	able to	breakable
-ance	state, condition, or action	acceptance
-en	to cause to be	dampen
-ful	full of, likely to	restful
-ish	being like	childish
-less	without	humorless
-ly	like, in the manner of	usually
-ment	the act of or result	government
-ous	full of	dangerous
-tion	the act of	invitation
-y	like or tending to	sticky

Prefixes and suffixes may be added to **root words** in order to make new words. If you know the meaning of a root word, and you know the meaning of a prefix or suffix, you can usually figure out the meaning of new words.

Many common root words come from Greek and Latin words, too. For example, the Greek word demos means "people." If you know that cracy means "rule," it's easy to understand why democracy means "rule by the people."

Some Common Greek and Latin Roots

Root Word	Meaning	New Word	New Word Meaning
auto	self	automobile	self-moving
dict	say, speak	diction	the art of speaking correctly
elect	choose	election	an act of choosing
geo	earth	geography	writing about the earth
graph	write, draw	geography	writing about the earth
human	human	humanity	all people
meter	measure	metric	concerning measurement
sphere	ball-shaped object	hemisphere	half of something sphere-shaped

Guided Practice

Mayor Selkirk's bid for <u>reelection</u> has been stalled. This newspaper alerted the public last April to her <u>mismanagement</u> of our city. The most recent polls show that the people, too, are fed up with <u>substandard</u> government. We urge voters to cast their ballot for Paul Price next Tuesday.

The word <u>reelection</u> means _____.

   A choosing wrongly

   B being chosen again

   C making a poor speech

   D the act or result of speaking

> You know that the root <u>elect</u> has to do with choosing, so that eliminates choices C and D. You know also that the prefix *re-* means "again," not "wrongly." Put these together with the suffix *-ion,* "an act of," and you know that choice B is the correct answer.

What does <u>substandard</u> mean?

   A up to standard   **C** beyond standard

   B below standard   **D** meeting many standards

> The tone of the passage, as well as its words, tells you how the author feels about Mayor Selkirk. You may also know the prefix *sub-* from words like *submarine* and *subway,* and you know it doesn't mean "up to," "beyond," or "many." So you probably didn't even have to look at the prefix chart to know that the correct answer is choice B.

What does <u>mismanagement</u> mean?

_____

> A look at the charts shows you that the prefix *mis-* means "bad," and the suffix *-ment* means "the act or result of." Your answer might be something like:

Management means "the act of managing badly."

Test Yourself

Ever hear of a dinosaur called *Manospondylus gigas?* Probably not. It's an <u>obscure</u> name even to scientists. Ever hear of *Tyrannosaurus rex?* Of course you have. *T. rex* is the most famous dinosaur of all. But some scientists believe he's been going about under an <u>alias</u>. *M. Gigas* may be his true name.

The question is: which was discovered first? <u>Customarily</u>, a scientist who first discovers a species gets to name it. Way back in 1892, a paleontologist named Edward Cope was working with a team of <u>geologists</u> in South Dakota. They dug up some bones of a dinosaur he called *Manospondylus gigas.* But he didn't find very much of the animal. So the name he gave it didn't <u>stick</u>. Ten years later, another scientist dug up a nearly complete skeleton of the same creature. It was named *Tyrannosaurus rex.*

Now jump ahead to the year 2000. That summer, some *T. rex* bones were <u>exhumed</u> in South Dakota. It turns out that they may be part of the very same animal that Cope found in 1892. According to the rules, his name has <u>priority</u>.

Could the name *T. rex* be on its way to becoming, well, *extinct?* "I don't believe so," one scientist commented. "It will be very hard to prove that this is part of Cope's animal. And even if it is, the rules may have to <u>bend</u>. The name *T. rex.* is part of our culture. Every kid knows it. The <u>public</u> will never call it by another name."

1 The word <u>obscure</u> means _____.

A famous

B difficult

C meat-eating

D little known

2 What is an <u>alias</u>?

A a skeleton

B a nickname

C a false name

D a dark cloud

3 Customarily means ____.

    A like a custom

    B against custom

    C according to custom

    D as a result of custom

4 Geologists are scientists who study ____.

    A the earth

    B dinosaurs

    C rain forests

    D human behavior

5 Explain your answer to question 4.

_____

_____

_____

_____

_____

6 In the second paragraph, the word stick means ____.

    A to stay close

    B a piece of wood

    C to last a long time

    D to pierce with something sharp

7 The word exhumed means ____.

    A burned

    B cut in pieces

    C put on display

    D dug out of the ground

8 What does <u>priority</u> mean in the third paragraph?

   A   an award

   B   a better sound

   C   the position of being first

   D   the quality of being harder to spell

9 As used in this article, the word <u>bend</u> means _____.

   A   to bow

   B   to curve or be crooked

   C   a part that is not straight

   D   to give way or move in a new direction

10 Explain your answer to question 9.

_____

_____

_____

_____

_____

UNIT 1
Vocabulary Development

Word Relationships

L.5.5, RL.5.4, RI.5.4

Words can have many shades of meaning. For example, just look at that last sentence. "Shades" is one of those words with multiple meanings. It can mean something you put over windows. It can mean lightness or darkness of color, as in shades of blue. It can even mean sunglasses. But what connection can it have with words?

Figurative Language

When we say that words have shades of meaning, we are using **figurative language.** Writers use figurative language to appeal to your senses in lively ways. It helps you see, feel, hear, or understand things more vividly. "The sun was hot" is a literal statement that simply tells you about the weather. "The sun beat down like a hammer" lets you *feel* how hot it was. "The sun was a conqueror without mercy" lets you feel it in an even more attention-getting way. How hot is *that?*

"The sun beat down like a hammer" is one type of figurative language, called a **simile** (SIM•uh•lee). A simile uses the word *like* or *as* to compare things that are very different from one another. This simile lets you feel the hot sun as something hard and oppressive.

A **metaphor** (MET•uh•for) is another type of figurative language. It compares two different things without using *like* or *as*. An example of a metaphor is that first sentence at the top of the page. It helps you see that the meanings of words can have shading much as colors do.

"The sun was a conqueror without mercy" is another type of figurative language called **personification.** The writer makes something natural or human-made—in this case, the sun—seem like a person in some way.

You need to be able to recognize and understand figurative language as you read. Otherwise, you might be puzzled about how words can have colors or how the sun can be like a carpenter's tool!

Elements of Poetry

Poetry often contains figurative language. It is one of the ways that poetry creates word pictures and sound effects in your mind. A poem's theme—the idea that the poet wants you to understand—is often expressed in figurative language.

There are many different kinds of poems. A **narrative poem** tells a story. A **lyric poem** mainly expresses feelings. Within these categories, there are many kinds of poems. A **sonnet,** for example, is a lyric poem in a regular 14-line form. A **ballad** is a narrative poem that was originally written to be sung.

Every poem has a **speaker.** The speaker in the poem expresses its ideas and represents the poet's point of view.

Many poems have **rhyme**—repeated sounds at the ends of words. Sometimes the rhyme comes at the ends of a line of poetry, as, for example, in this **limerick,** a humorous five-line poem:

> The inventor, he chuckled with **glee**
> As they fished his airship from the **sea.**
> "I shall build"—and he **laughed,**
> "A submarine **craft,**
> "And perhaps it will fly!" remarked **he.**

Sometimes rhyming words appear in the same line:

> Jack and **Jill** went up the **hill**
> To fetch a pail of water;
> Jack fell **down** and broke his **crown...**

And many poems have no rhyme at all, as for example in this **haiku,** a three-line poem of 17 syllables:

> Canada geese land
> on the storm-soaked baseball field;
> feet first they slide—safe!

Rhythm is the pattern of stressed or unstressed beats in a line of poetry. A stressed beat has more force than an unstressed beat.

> A **bird** came **down** the **walk**—
> He **did** not **know** I **saw**;
> He **bit** an **angleworm** in **halves**
> And **ate** the **fellow**, **raw**.

Some poems have neither rhyme nor a regular rhythm. Poems like these are called **free verse.**

> When it is finally ours, this freedom, this liberty, this beautiful
> and terrible thing, needful to man as air,
> usable as earth; when it belongs at last to all...

Besides using figurative language, poets also add meaning by using the *sounds* of words in playful ways. **Alliteration** is the repetition of the same, or very similar, beginning consonant sounds in a line of poetry. In this line, the /s/ sound is an example of alliteration:

> *Serving supper to sailors, salting their meat...*

Onomatopoeia is another way that poets play with sound. Words that imitate the sound of something, such as *bang, whiz,* and *meow* are examples of onomatopoeia.

A poem may be divided into **stanzas**—groups of lines separated by spaces. The poem on the next page is in two stanzas.

Guided Practice

A Day

by Emily Dickinson

I'll tell you how the sun rose,
A ribbon at a time.
The steeples swam in amethyst[1],
The news like squirrels ran.
5   The hills untied their bonnets,
The bobolinks[2] begun.
Then I said softly to myself,
"That must have been the sun!"

But how he set, I know not.
10   There seemed a purple stile[3]
Which little yellow boys and girls
Were climbing all the while
Till when they reached the other side,
A dominie[4] in gray
15   Put gently up the evening bars,
And led the flock away.

Which line in the poem includes a simile?

A   A ribbon at a time

B   The news like squirrels ran.

C   There seemed a purple stile

D   And led the flock away.

> Dickinson uses a lot of figurative language in this poem. But there is only one simile: in line 4, where she describes the "news" of the sunrise as running quickly, *like* squirrels. None of the other choices compare two things by using *like* or *as*. The answer is choice B.

---

[1]**amethyst:** purple

[2]**bobolinks:** a kind of bird

[3]**stile:** step or set of steps for climbing over a wall or fence

[4]**dominie:** church minister or teacher

In line 2, what is the speaker comparing with ribbons?

A the horizon

B the sun's rays

C her window blinds

D plowed rows in a field

> Dickinson uses "ribbons" to describe something about the way the sun rose, so you know it isn't about anything indoors or on the ground. Have you ever been up early enough to see the sun rise? Then you know that the sun's rays can look like thin streaks. Dickinson uses metaphor when she calls these streaks "ribbons." Choice B is correct.

"The hills untied their bonnets" is an example of ____.

A a simile

B metaphor

C onomatopoeia

D personification

> Here Dickinson continues her image of "ribbons." As the sun climbs higher, there are more streaks, and the colors are getting brighter. She is not comparing the hills with anything directly (choice A or B) or playing with sound (choice C), but she does make you see the hills as women untying the ribbons on their bonnets. Did you notice, too, that in line 9 she calls the sun "he"? Both are examples of personification, choice D.

Write a line from the poem that uses alliteration.

_____

_____

> Alliteration is the repetition of a consonant sound in a line of poetry. Here is a sample answer:

Dickinson uses alliteration with the /s/ sound in line 3, "The steeples swam in amethyst."

In the second stanza, what might the stile and the yellow boys and girls be?

_____

_____

> ✓ There is no single correct answer to a question like this. It all depends on how you interpret the poem. Read the question carefully. Make sure you understand what it is asking you to do. This question asks you to interpret some of the poet's colorful metaphors. Try to picture in your mind the scene the poet describes. Here is one sample answer:

The stile is a metaphor for low clouds on the horizon, and the yellow children are the sun's rays as it sets.

Idioms, Adages, and Proverbs

Idioms are another kind of figurative language. An idiom is a phrase in which the words are not related to their actual meanings. For example, you catch a cold, but the meaning of the phrase has nothing to do with the literal meanings of *catch* or *cold*.

Here are some other familiar idioms:

Idiom	Meaning
come clean	tell the truth
crazy about	liking very much
slam dunk	something very easy
freeze up	become too nervous to do a task

Idioms usually start out as metaphors. Then they become so much a part of our language that we understand them without thinking of the literal meaning of the words. For example, slam dunk is a term from the game of basketball. Today someone might say, "That spelling test was a slam dunk," meaning "easy," even if they know nothing about basketball.

What are some other idioms you can think of? Write a few on the lines below.

Idiom   **Meaning**

_____   _____

_____   _____

_____   _____

_____   _____

   Adages and **proverbs** are short "wise sayings" that have been used in a culture for a long time. Most proverbs start out as metaphors, too. When they have repeated enough times that everyone understands them without thinking of their literal meaning, they become adages. For example, you may have heard people say, "Don't count your chickens until they hatch." That's an adage that means "Don't expect something good to happen until it actually does."

   Here are some other familiar adages and proverbs. Can you see the metaphor in each of them?

Adage or Proverb	Meaning
When the cat's away, the mice will play.	When the person in charge is not looking, others will act irresponsibly.
You can't judge a book by its cover.	You can't tell what a person is really like by how he or she looks.
Well begun is half done.	The most important step in a task is to start.
A new broom sweeps clean.	A fresh leader brings in new ideas.

Write a few more adages and proverbs that you have heard.

Adage or Proverb   **Meaning**

_____   _____

_____   _____

_____   _____

_____   _____

Guided Practice

Read the passage. Then answer the questions.

"I thought Jennifer was my friend!" Amy was in tears. "Now I find out she's been <u>talking trash</u> about me behind my back! She's nothing but <u>a wolf in sheep's clothing!</u>"

"People who live in glass houses shouldn't throw stones," Haley said. "Don't you ever gossip about people? I've heard you making fun of the clothes Jennifer wears."

"Well, yes, but that's a horse of a different color," Amy sniffed.

"You really think so?" said Haley. "Maybe you ought to <u>walk a mile in her shoes.</u>"

What does the idiom <u>talking trash</u> mean in this passage?

A lying

B bragging

C insulting

D talking about an unpleasant topic

> Talking trash is a relatively new idiom in our language. Think of the metaphor that may be suggested by the word *trash*. The context doesn't suggest lies or bragging, or an unpleasant topic, any of which may be suggested by *trash*, but it clearly shows that here the idiom means "insulting." Choice C is correct.

<u>A wolf in sheep's clothing</u> is an idiom that means _____.

A a strong person who acts weak

B an enemy who pretends to be a friend

C a person who should not be taken seriously

D someone who doesn't care what others think

> The idiom <u>a wolf in sheep's clothing</u> comes from one of Aesop's fables. The wolf dresses up as a sheep to win their trust in order to get close enough to eat them. Think of the images the words *wolf* and *sheep* suggest—a predator and a mild, gentle animal—and you can eliminate all the choices but one. You could probably also infer from the context that choice B is the answer you want.

UNIT 1 ▓▓▓▓▓▓▓▓▓▓▓▓▓▓▓▓▓▓▓▓▓▓▓▓▓▓▓▓
Vocabulary Development

What does the adage <u>walk a mile in her shoes</u> mean?

_____

_____

✓ Here again, the context tells you what the adage means. Amy gossips about other people, but she hasn't thought about how that makes them feel until she is the object of gossip. Here is a sample answer:

"To walk a mile in her shoes" means to put yourself in her place and imagine how she feels.

What are two other adages or proverbs in the passage? Explain what they mean.

_____

_____

_____

✓ You probably identified "People who live in glass houses shouldn't throw stones" and "A horse of a different color" as phrases that don't really have to do with stones or horses. Here is a sample answer:

The first adage means, "Don't wrong a person if you can be wronged the same way." The second means "another thing entirely" or "something else."

Word Relationships

Sometimes you can better understand the shades of meaning between words by considering their **synonyms, antonyms,** and **homographs.**

Make sure you know the exact meaning and pronunciation of these synonyms by looking them up in a print or online dictionary.

You know that **synonyms** are words that have almost the same meaning. But there can be a lot of difference in that "almost." Consider the adjective <u>thrifty</u>. It describes a person who is careful about spending money. No one would be offended by being called thrifty. But now consider these synonyms: <u>tight</u>, <u>cheap</u>, <u>stingy</u>, <u>miserly</u>. How would you feel about a person described by any of those words?

Antonyms are words that have opposite meanings to one another. Again consider <u>thrifty</u> and its synonyms as you read these sentences:

> He was so <u>profligate</u> with the fortune he inherited that it was gone within a year.
>
> He was so <u>generous</u> with the fortune he inherited that every charity in town was soon calling him.

Both <u>profligate</u> and <u>generous</u> describe someone who is careless about spending money. But think about what they mean in terms of their opposites. <u>Profligate</u> is an antonym of <u>thrifty</u>. It has the sense of being foolish or wasteful. <u>Generous</u> can be said to be an antonym of <u>tight</u>, <u>cheap</u>, <u>stingy</u>, or <u>miserly</u>. It describes what most people would consider a positive quality.

Homographs are words that are spelled the same but have different meanings and sometimes different pronunciation. They may not even have anything to do with one another, such as a <u>nail</u> on your finger and a <u>nail</u> that you pound with a hammer. It's important not to confuse a word with its homograph when you read it in a sentence—such as in this poem:

Word Twins

by Karen Stamfil

Words have their own lives, each its tale telling
    when we speak its name.
For every sense and sound, a different spelling
    —except when they're the same!
5 The farmer <u>sows</u> his field, then feeds his <u>sows</u>.
The doctor <u>wound</u> a bandage 'round a <u>wound</u>.
Don't <u>close</u> the door—we're all too <u>close</u> together!
Happy birthday—let me <u>present</u> this <u>present</u>!
Such word twins are the <u>subject</u> of my rhyme
10   —but I'll protect you:
To more such interruptions of your time
    I'll not <u>subject</u> you!

UNIT 1
Vocabulary Development

Guided Practice

Which word would *best* replace <u>thought</u> in this sentence?

Emma thought that the man in the baseball cap was the one who had stolen her bicycle.

A knew

B believed

C suspected

D understood

> All these verbs represent different degrees of thinking. Emma doesn't really *know* that the man stole her bike, but her thinking goes beyond *belief* or *understanding.* Choice C, <u>suspected</u>, is the best answer.

Which word is an antonym of <u>ill</u> in this sentence?

Mack was sorry for having once thought ill of Ms. Arunas.

A well

B healthy

C friendly

D pleasantly

> "Healthy" can be an antonym for <u>ill</u> in a different context. But here <u>ill</u> describes Mack's feelings toward someone else, not his health. The most precisely opposite word is <u>well</u>, choice A.

Explain the homographs in this sentence.

My brother <u>ragged</u> on me for wearing my favorite <u>ragged</u> T-shirt.

_____

_____

_____

> Here is one way to answer the question:
>
> The first <u>ragged</u> is a verb. It has one syllable and means "made fun of." The second <u>ragged</u> is an adjective. It has two syllables and means "torn and tattered."

Test Yourself

From the moment I walked in, I was <u>sorry</u> I had come. The vast room was a temple of forgotten and forgettable reading. It was an old hangar. The navy had parked and fixed <u>planes</u> there through three wars. That morning it felt as though they hadn't had the heat turned on since 1945. The stacks of books on the tables seemed like the towers of an enemy fortress.

"You took your sweet time getting here." Joe Buxton's voice boomed out of the darkness. I squinted. My scoutmaster stood at the end of a long aisle, tables laden with books on either side. Now I could make out the other boys grouped around him—Thanen, Kyle, Antonio, all members of my patrol. All six of them. My cheeks burned.

"I didn't think it was important to be here right on the dot," I muttered.

"Well, you're here now," Joe said. "I didn't want Ms. Lettieri here to have to repeat her instructions. Donna?"

A woman stepped forward from the shadows. In her overalls, she looked like a farm wife dressed for a day of pitching hay.

"Thank you, Mr. Buxton, and thank you, boys, for volunteering," the woman said brightly. "You may not know that the Friends of the Library sale is one of the chief ways that the library system has to raise money. The adult volunteers have already organized the books by category—fiction, history, art, and so on. Your <u>job</u> is to pack them all in boxes and set them out under the correct signs for tomorrow's sale. If you have any questions about where something should go, please don't guess! Ask me!"

"Well, let's get started," Joe said in the hearty voice he used to raise our spirits on 15-mile hikes. "'Many hands make light work,' my grandmother always said."

1 In the first sentence, the narrator feels <u>sorry</u> for having come. A better synonym for the way he feels would be _____.

A sad

B bitter

C regretful

D remorseful

UNIT 1 :::
Vocabulary Development

2 When the narrator calls the hangar "a temple of forgotten and forgettable reading," the author wants you to understand that ____.

    A it was as quiet as a library

    B it seemed like a religious place to him

    C Thomas doesn't care much about reading

    D there were more books than he had ever seen in one place

3 "The stacks of books on the tables seemed like the towers of an enemy fortress." In this sentence, the author shows you how the narrator feels by using ____.

    A a simile

    B a metaphor

    C onomatopoeia

    D personification

4 In the second paragraph, what does the idiom <u>make out</u> mean?

    A see

    B survive

    C understand

    D feel happy about

5 What is an idiom in the passage that means <u>on time</u>?

_____

_____

_____

_____

_____

6 Explain a metaphor in the passage that shows that the narrator was embarrassed?

_____

_____

_____

_____

_____

7 In the first paragraph, how can you tell that the word <u>planes</u> means "flying machines" and not "flat surfaces"?

_____

_____

_____

_____

_____

8 Ms. Lettieri calls what the boys are doing a "job." What synonym might the narrator use for it?

_____

_____

_____

_____

_____

9 Explain the adage the narrator uses in the last paragraph.

_____

_____

_____

_____

_____

32

UNIT 1 ▨▨▨▨▨▨▨▨▨▨▨▨▨▨▨▨▨▨▨▨▨▨▨▨▨▨▨▨▨▨▨▨▨▨▨
Vocabulary Development

Content-Specific Words

As you read, you notice different levels of words. First, there are the words you use in ordinary conversation. Second, there are the words that you may not use when you speak but that you encounter when you read. Some of these words represent the shades of meaning and more exact ways of saying things that you learned about in Lessons 1 and 2—words like *dwelling, alacrity,* and *profligate.* You might run across words like these in any kind of text, from fiction to biographies to newspaper articles.

Then there are words that are specific to certain kinds of reading. For example, you wouldn't ordinarily have to understand words like *magma* or *eruption,* but you would if you were reading about volcanoes. *Emancipation* and *ordnance* are not everyday words either. But if you were reading about the American Civil War of 1861–1865, you might get confused if you didn't understand them. Fortunately, you can use the same kinds of context clues to understand words like these as you do when learning any new words.

Guided Practice

Read the passage. Then answer the questions.

Your Amazing Chemical Factory

by Einar F. Klamst

There's a chemical factory in your body. It's on the right side of your <u>abdomen</u>, guarded by your rib cage. It makes chemicals that your body needs to <u>digest</u> food. It processes and stores the <u>nutrients</u> from the food you eat. Then it <u>processes</u> them again when your body needs them for energy. It breaks down poisons. It does about 500 jobs, many of which science doesn't completely understand. This amazing factory is your liver.

The liver makes a greenish liquid called bile. The body stores it in the gall bladder and releases it into the intestines during digestion. Bile breaks down fats into smaller <u>molecules</u> that your cells can use. Other chemicals in the liver help carry them to the cells.

Every minute, about three-tenths of your blood flows through your liver. Some of it brings in oxygen from your heart. But most of it comes through the *portal vein.* This vein carries nutrients and waste products from your intestines for the liver to process.

> With a small group, research and prepare a presentation on one of the jobs that your liver does. Use this article and the illustration as a starting point for your research.

UNIT 1
Vocabulary Development

33

The liver <u>converts</u> the nutrients into molecules that your body needs for growth, energy, and repairing cells. It stores energy in a large molecule called *glycogen*. When you need extra energy, the liver breaks glycogen down into a form your muscle cells can use to produce it.

The liver is your poison-control center. It breaks down <u>toxic</u> chemicals and converts them to harmless ones to be passed out of the body. But some poisons <u>overwhelm</u> the liver. The poisons in some mushrooms can stop its working completely. Alcohol, too, damages the liver. It causes fat deposits that slow the flow of blood.

The liver makes chemicals that help wounds to heal. It makes chemicals that help your body fight diseases. It removes chemicals that can cause brain damage. You can see why it's important to take care of your body's chemical factory.

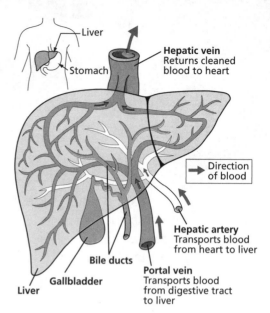

What is a more common word for <u>abdomen</u>?

A head

B belly

C pelvis

D muscles

> **Abdomen** is a word that you might come across in ordinary reading, not just in a science article. But if you don't know what it means, the phrase "guarded by your rib cage" is a clue. You know it can't be your head, pelvis, or muscles. Your abdomen is your belly. Choice B is the correct answer.

To <u>digest</u> food means to ____.

A eat in an unhealthy way

B pass waste products out of the body

C change it so that the body can absorb it

D get it from your mouth to your stomach

> **Digest** is a word that could come up in conversation, especially around the dinner table. But the passage uses it in a more scientific way. You might be able to tell from the context that it's a process that happens *after* you've eaten (choice A), and that choices B and D describe *parts* of the process of digestion. But choice C defines all of it, and is the correct answer.

What does <u>toxic</u> mean?

    A natural

    B complex

    C necessary

    D poisonous

> Here is a word that has a specific, scientific meaning. Again the context provides a clue as to what it means. The subject of paragraph 5 is poisons. It describes how the liver breaks down some poisons but can be damaged by others. Choice D is the answer you want.

Write definitions for the other underlined words in the passage. If you can't tell the meaning of the word from the context, look it up in a print or online dictionary.

nutrients   _____

processes (verb)   _____

molecules   _____

converts (verb)   _____

overwhelm   _____

> Did you get them all? Your answers might read something like these:

      nutrients—chemicals your body needs for health

      processes—sets of actions in a special order

      molecules—small particles of matter

      converts—changes

      overwhelm—to defeat completely

Visiting Plimoth Plantation

by Niles Binford

Want to meet a Pilgrim? Care to visit the <u>site</u> where "the first Thanksgiving" was celebrated? You can (sort of), and you won't need a time machine to do it. You only need to spend a day at Plimoth Plantation.

Plimoth Plantation is located about two and a half miles from the site of the actual colonial village of the 1620s. That site lies buried under the modern town of Plymouth, Massachusetts. Plimoth Plantation is a historical theme park. It's one of several places around our country where role players in costume re-enact historical <u>eras</u> and events. Walk through the gate of the high wooden <u>palisade</u>, and you're in an English village of 1627. Stroll among the houses, barns, shops, and animal pens. You'll see the men and women of the village about their daily tasks. Go ahead and talk to them. That's what they're there for. They speak in a 17th-century English <u>dialect</u>, but it's not hard to understand. Ask them about their lives and work. Only don't call them "pilgrims." They'll look at you quizzically. The Plymouth colonists did not use that word for themselves. It only became popular in histories written 200 years later. And don't ask about "the first Thanksgiving," either. They won't know what you mean. Oh, they may tell you about the harvest festival of 1621 that they celebrated with the Indians. But don't expect them to have much good to say about the "Native Americans." (That's another term that will confuse them.) They'll express the <u>intolerance</u> the English settlers generally had toward native people and their ways.

As for the Indians, they're here, too. Just downhill from the English village, by the water's edge, is the homesite of the Wampanoag, the <u>indigenous</u> people of the region. You'll find traditional Wampanoag *wetus*, dome-shaped houses covered with bark or reeds. The native people are not actors and do not role-play. Most are actual Wampanoag, while others come from native communities across the United States. They'll talk to you about customs and demonstrate crafts native to the Wampanoag.

A five-minute drive away, you'll find the *Mayflower II*, a full-scale <u>replica</u> of the sailing ship that brought the real Plymouth colonists to Massachusetts. That's part of the exhibit, too. Walk through the ship, talk to the sailors, and observe <u>maritime</u> artisans at work on shipboard crafts. When your touring is done, you may want to step back into the 21st century for a treat at the ice-cream parlor across the street.

1 In the first paragraph, the word <u>site</u> is a synonym for ____.

    A sight

    B town

    C location

    D building

2 In the second paragraph, the word <u>eras</u> means ____.

    A actors

    B mistakes

    C time periods

    D famous people

3 As used in this article, a <u>palisade</u> is a ____.

    A church

    B high cliff

    C protective wall

    D hall built for entertainment

4 A <u>dialect</u> is a ____.

    A secret code

    B conversation

    C form of a language

    D script used by actors

5 In paragraph 3, the word <u>indigenous</u> is a synonym for ____.

    A clever

    B native

    C Indian

    D costumed

6 A <u>replica</u> is a _____.

    A ship

    B copy

    C stage for a play

    D map or diagram

7 What does <u>intolerance</u> mean?

_____

_____

_____

_____

_____

8 What does <u>maritime</u> mean?

_____

_____

_____

_____

_____

REVIEW

Vocabulary Development

Read the passage. Then answer the questions.

The Revenge of Albus

by Mark Falstein

My neighbors' cat, Albus, is fat. Not sleek. Not plump. Fat. This is a cat who likes his Friskies and who is probably <u>indulged</u> with table scraps as well. Albus is a well-contented feline, as white and blubbery as a polar bear in summer. You see the other neighborhood cats on their daily rounds, stalking real or imagined prey. You see them watching the squirrels that scamper along the maple branches, following them with their eyes with no hope of catching them. Sometimes they bring an <u>unfortunate</u> trophy home to their humans. Not Albus. He probably never caught a mouse in his life. He likes nothing better than to lie on the roof of his house, a couple doors down the hill from mine, and sleep in the sun. How he manages to haul his 25 pounds up there is a wonder of nature, but he does it. He's a good-natured slob, which is probably what led that blue jay to think he could bully him for so long.

A bird geek friend of mine told me that this feathered citizen is more properly called a Steller's jay. By me he's a common blue jay, of the same species Mark Twain said could out-swear any other critter. I don't know where his nest was, but that summer he <u>staked out his turf</u> in the cedar tree directly above Albus's roof. From there he cussed out Albus, Albus's mother, and all cat-kind day after day, for hours on end. He would swoop down at Albus, screaming his insults, fly back up to another branch, and do it again. And again. Always he stayed safely out of Albus's reach. Every bully is a coward, as we all know.

But if the jay was a coward, what did that make Albus? As the summer went on, I actually found myself feeling embarrassed for the cat. Why didn't he stick up for himself? Why didn't he at least snarl back like a self-respecting predator—do something, *anything,* to stop the abuse? What was he, a cat or a…mouse?

But where there's a will, there's a way. As it turned out, Albus was just biding his time. He was contented and lazy, but he was also cagey. He knew just how far he could lunge and reach without having to work too hard at it. And, at last, there came the morning when the screaming jay got just a little too cocky, a little too close.

Zap! Without wasting a move, Albus lashed out with one paw and caught the jay's tail feathers. The bird let out a screech that might have been heard in the next time zone. You could actually see him pump up his wings in terror, like a bird in a cartoon, as he escaped into the cedar's high branches.

I don't believe Albus did him any harm. He's a good-natured sort, after all, and only wanted to enjoy his rooftop naps in peace. But that jay never hassled him again, and I'm convinced that it was a smirk of satisfaction that I saw cross Albus's jowls.

1 Which of these words is a synonym for <u>indulged</u>?

   A fed

   B petted

   C spoiled

   D tolerated

2 The author uses several synonyms for <u>overweight</u> in talking about Albus. If a cat had human feelings, which one would Albus *probably* prefer to be called?

   A fat

   B plump

   C sleek

   D blubbery

3 <u>Fortunate</u> is a synonym for *lucky*. What does <u>unfortunate</u> mean in paragraph 1?

   A not lucky

   B lucky once

   C lucky again

   D more than lucky

4 <u>Staked out his turf</u> is an idiom that means ____.

   A built a nest

   B stayed hidden

   C claimed his territory

   D kept watch over the area

5 The idiom <u>biding his time</u> means ____.

   A waiting

   B making plans

   C getting stronger

   D gaining courage

6 The word <u>cagey</u> means ____.

   A free

   B quick

   C tricky

   D courageous

7 In paragraph 1, what is a simile the author uses to help the reader visualize Albus?

_____

_____

_____

_____

_____

8 Explain the adage "Where there's a will, there's a way" in paragraph 4.

_____

_____

_____

_____

_____

To the Thawing Wind

by Robert Frost

Come with rain, O loud Southwester!
Bring the singer, bring the nester;
Give the buried flower a dream;
Make the settled snowbank steam;
5   Find the brown beneath the white;
But whate'er you do tonight,
Bathe my window, make it flow,
Melt it as the ice will go;
Melt the glass and leave the sticks
10 Like a hermit's crucifix;
Burst into my narrow stall;
Swing the picture on the wall;
Run the rattling pages o'er;
Scatter poems on the floor;
15 Turn the poet out of door.

9 In this poem's central metaphor, the southwest wind stands for _____.

    A the coming of spring

    B the poems the poet writes

    C a woman the speaker loves

    D things the speaker wants to do

10 Explain three lines that support your answer to question 9.

_____

_____

_____

_____

_____

There's a popular saying in Chicago: "If you don't like our weather, wait five minutes." They say the same thing in San Francisco, Buffalo, and a lot of other places. Everywhere, it seems, people like to talk about the weather, joke about the weather, and complain about the weather. As for the <u>meteorologists</u> who tell us what tomorrow's weather will be—well, what do *they* know?

Actually, they know a great deal. Many people think the weather is <u>unpredictable</u>. <u>In the long run</u>, that's true. There are too many <u>variables</u>. Weather results from the <u>interaction</u> of the sun, air, oceans, and land. A weather system may cover several states or a single city block. It may move quickly or stay in one place for months. But most weather systems follow regular patterns. By studying computer data and photos taken from <u>satellites</u> in space, meteorologists can make accurate forecasts up to five days ahead. And within 24 hours, they are accurate more than nine times out of ten. Of course, that isn't much comfort if the tenth time happens to be the day you're planning your picnic!

11 What are <u>meteorologists</u>?

   A scientists who study meteors

   B scientists who study weather

   C people who report the weather on TV

   D people who are wrong about the weather

12 An <u>unpredictable</u> event is one that _____.

   A will not happen

   B someone can cause to happen

   C happens after someone says it will

   D one cannot say will happen before it does

13 <u>Variables</u> are _____.

   A numbers

   B different kinds

   C storm systems

   D things that can change

14 <u>Interaction</u> means _____.

   A between events

   B going out of control

   C acting upon each other

   D studying what has happened before

15 What does the idiom <u>in the long run</u> mean?

_____

_____

_____

_____

_____

16 In the context of this passage, what are <u>satellites</u>?

_____

_____

_____

_____

_____

Key Ideas and Details

There are many kinds of things to read. You read literature for enjoyment—books that tell stories, poems, even plays written to be performed on a stage. You read informational texts to find out about history, science, art, and many other things. You read functional texts such as bus schedules and advertisements. You read these things in print form and on computers and other electronic media. But whatever text you're reading, you're reading about ideas and details. Ideas and details and the connections among them make up the fabric of a text.

This unit is all about those ideas and details. As you read, you need to be able to remember details, to identify which are the important ones, and to understand how they relate to one another.

- **In Lesson 4,** you'll learn about details and how to recall them accurately to explain what a text says. You'll learn how to identify details that are stated directly in a text and those that may take a little figuring out.

- **Lesson 5** is about the ideas that the details support. You'll learn how to identify the main idea of a text—the answer to the question "What's it about?"—and the other important ideas and details that support the main idea. And you'll learn how to summarize a text—to explain briefly what it's about, referring only to the most important ideas and details.

- **Lesson 6** is about the connections between ideas and details in literary texts. You learned something about the elements of poetry in Lesson 2. In this lesson, you'll learn about the elements of stories and plays. You'll learn how to identify key details about the characters, events, and settings in a literary text and how they interconnect with one another to tell a story.

- **Lesson 7** is about the connections between ideas and details in informational texts. Just as characters, events, and places work together to tell a story, so do people, events, and ideas relate to one another to give you insights about such subjects as events in history or processes in science. You'll learn how to recognize these connections in what you read, and to use them to better understand what you're reading about.

Understanding a Text

RL.5.1, RI.5.1

Vocabulary
abolitionist

allegedly

featured

Underground
Railroad

What makes a book interesting? One difference you may have noticed between a good book and a dull one is the details. Good books have a lot of details. It's the details that enliven a book, whether they're details about how a character in a story behaves or about a discovery in science. That's why **noting and recalling details** as you read is important. If you just "skim" what you're reading, you won't get the details. You may miss something important, or even become confused about what you're reading. See how many details you can remember as you read the article below about a favorite author.

Guided Practice

Read the passage. Then answer the questions.

Reading did not come easy for Beverly Bunn. Until she was old enough for school, she lived on a farm near Yamhill, Oregon. The town was so small that it didn't even have a library. So her mother arranged for books to be sent there from a state library. They were kept in a room over a bank, and Beverly's mother became a sort of librarian.

featured
gave an important place to

Beverly learned to love books. But when she was 6 years old, her family moved to Portland, Oregon's largest city. She was placed in the lowest reading group in first grade. City air did not agree with her after her years on the farm. She often had to miss school, which set her even further behind. By the third grade, however, she had caught up. She had discovered stories in which "something was actually happening." She enjoyed reading so much that her school librarian suggested that she might want to write books for children when she grew up.

Beverly attended college in California. After earning a degree in library science, she got a job as a children's librarian in Yakima, Washington. Part of her job was leading the "story hour," reading books to young children. They asked for stories in which the kids were "like us," and Beverly couldn't find any. So after she married Clarence Cleary, she began to write them. They were funny stories about the neighborhoods and towns where she had lived, where kids had adventures with their dogs and rode home-built scooters.

Beverly's first book was published in 1950. *Henry Huggins* and its sequels were popular with children from the start. Then a few years later, one of her young readers asked her why none of her leading characters had any brothers or sisters. So she made up an annoying little sister for one of her characters. She gave this terrible 2-year-old the name Ramona—Ramona Geraldine Quimby.

It was Ramona, of course, who made Beverly Cleary one of the most successful writers of her day. She has written more than 30 books for children and teens, and no fewer than seven have featured Ramona. By the time the most recent one, *Ramona's World,* was published in 1999, Cleary's star character had made it to age 9. Beverly Cleary, still writing, made it to age 94 in 2010.

> Find a list of Beverly Cleary's books on the Internet. Make a tally of how many students in your class have read each of them. Which is the most popular among your classmates?

Where did Beverly Cleary spend her earliest years?

A   on a farm

B   in California

C   in Portland, Oregon

D   in a room over a bank

> Were you reading carefully? All of these places played a role in Beverly's life. But it's a key detail of her early life and experience with books that she grew up in a place without a library. The first paragraph tells you directly that it wasn't in California, Portland, or over a bank. Choice A is the correct answer.

Who first suggested to Beverly that she write children's books?

A   her mother

B   her husband

C   a school librarian

D   her third-grade teacher

> Details like this are important because they give you insights about a person, fictional character, or event. You can guess that the person who inspired Beverly to write for children deeply influenced her life. The last sentence of the second paragraph tells you that you can give credit not to her mother, husband, or teacher, but to a school librarian. Choice C is the correct answer.

Where did Beverly get ideas for her early stories?

_____

_____

No doubt Beverly Cleary has always had an active imagination and was influenced by the books she enjoyed as a child. But any writer—even a writer of fantasy—bases her material on what she knows, and in Beverly's case, the passage says so. One answer you might have written is suggested in the third paragraph:

Beverly got her ideas from children in the cities and towns where she had lived.

In which section of the library would you find Beverly Cleary's books?

A   fiction

B   history

C   reference

D   biography

You know the answer to this question even though none of these words appears anywhere in the passage. The question calls on you to **make an inference**—to combine information that you read with information that you already know to find details that are not directly stated. Beverly Cleary writes stories about characters she makes up, and you know that's fiction. History, reference books, and biography are all concerned with facts. Choice A is correct.

Why was Beverly placed in the lowest reading group in first grade?

_____

_____

> ✓ This is another question that you have to answer by inference. The second paragraph says that she had a hard time adjusting to "city air" and often had to miss school, so you can infer that she was sick much of the time. But a more important detail is in the second half of that paragraph: she had caught up by the third grade because she had discovered stories in which "something was actually happening." Here is a sample answer:

Beverly fell behind because she was bored with the books she was given to read.

Read the passage. Then answer the questions.

Let Us Give Thanks!

by Karen Stamfil

Don't get the wrong idea—we had plenty to be thankful for that week. Dad's operation had been successful. The doctors said he should make a complete recovery. But meanwhile he would have to stay in the hospital through Thanksgiving and a few days beyond, and he would be eating through tubes for a while. Mom was a nervous wreck. She tended to regard an ordinary cold as if it were cancer, so it had taken a while to sink in just how serious Dad's infection really was. But she wasn't in any space to cook a big feast, and she was spending most of her time at the hospital with Dad besides. Aunt Lute had invited us to dinner, and so had the Alexanders down the street. We were debating those choices—Aunt Lute's pies versus the fun factor of spending the holiday with the Alexander kids—when my brother Chase, home from college, announced that he would cook Thanksgiving dinner.

✓ Turkey
✓ Sweet potatoes
✓ Bread
✓ Corn
✓ Green beans
✓ Cranberries
✓ Flour
✓ Sugar
✓ Butter
✓ Pumpkin
✓ Rolls

"Since when can you cook?" Dina asked doubtfully. She was 8 and wasn't very good yet at hiding what she was thinking.

"I happen to be a very good cook," Chase said. "There's nothing to it."

"Yeah, but have you ever cooked a turkey?" said Craig. At 16, he was halfway in age between Chase and me. "Not to mention cranberry sauce and gravy and—"

"That's what cookbooks are for," Chase said, dismissing Craig's concerns with an airy wave of his hand. "I'll make out a shopping list. Craig, you can take my car and do the shopping. Simone, you'll be my sous-chef, Dina can set the table, and you can leave everything else to me."

Chase was in his second year at Western State—a sophomore. You know what the word *sophomore* means? It means "wise fool." I'm not making that up. Chase is tall with black hair and a kind of drooping nose that makes him look like a bird peering down at the world from his perch. Maybe he had learned to cook, but I had been in the apartment he shared with three friends at the university, and what I mostly saw in their kitchen was pizza crust and empty pizza boxes. And ants.

"Right," I said. "What's a Sue chef?"

Chase gave me a wise-fool look. "It means an assistant cook. It's French. Don't worry, I'll tell you everything you need to do. Some people can even burn water," he added. It was a sentence that would live on in family legend for years to come.

What is the name of the narrator in the story?

A Lute

B Dina

C Simone

D Alexander

This is a "first-person" story, one in which the narrator is one of the characters. In stories like this, authors need a way of introducing the narrator's name. You can tell that the narrator isn't Dina, Aunt Lute, or anyone named Alexander, because she refers to them all by name. Chase tells someone named Simone that she will be his "sous-chef," and the narrator answers. The correct answer is choice C.

Why can't the children's mother cook Thanksgiving dinner?

    A   She is sick.

    B   She can't cook.

    C   She is out of town on business.

    D   Her husband just had an operation.

> The story takes off from the fact that the children's mother isn't able to cook dinner, so *why* is an important detail. Nowhere does the narrator suggest that her mother is sick, out of town, or a bad cook. You learn in the first paragraph that the children's father is in the hospital. The mother is spending a lot of time with him and is a "nervous wreck" besides. You can infer that choice D is the correct answer.

Which of these is *not* a detail that describes Chase?

    A   He is tall.

    B   He has black hair.

    C   He has brown eyes.

    D   He has a drooping nose.

> Simone describes her brother in paragraph 6, so that readers can picture him in their minds as the story develops. He is tall with black hair and a drooping nose. One detail Simone doesn't mention is the color of his eyes. Choice C is the correct answer.

About how old is Simone?

> This is another detail that helps you imagine a key character, but you have to make an inference to do it. Simone tells you that her 16-year-old-brother Craig is halfway in age between Chase and herself. Chase is in his second year of college, so you can infer that he's 19 or 20. A sample answer might be:

Simone is 12 or 13 years old.

What is the children's mother like? What is a detail in the story that gives you a clue?

_____

_____

_____

✓ The mother doesn't appear in this part of the story, but you know something about her from what Simone tells you. Simone may be exaggerating when she says that her mother "tended to regard an ordinary cold as if it were cancer." But it does suggest something about her mother. One answer could be:

> The children's mother is a worrier who in her mind makes things seem worse than they are. The clue is in Simone's comment about how her mother acts when someone has a cold.

It can be important to note details in advertising, too.

Read the advertisement. Then answer the questions.

"A hit for kids 8–80! Don't miss it!"
—Janice Vance, WLZC-FM

On-the-Boards Children's Theater presents...

The Boxcar Children

A play by Arianna Yeager
based on Gertrude Chandler Warner's beloved series

Performances Thursday through Sunday, September 27–November 4

Tickets Going Fast! **Call 1-888-555-3434,** or order online at **www.on-the-boards.org**

Special School Rates Available

Who is the author of the play that is advertised?

A Janice Vance

B Beverly Cleary

C Arianna Yeager

D Gertrude Chandler Warner

> ✓ Did you read the ad carefully? Janice Vance is quoted in the ad, and Beverly Cleary is nowhere mentioned. Gertrude Chandler Warner is the author of the *book series* the play is based on, but the play is "by Arianna Yeager." Choice C is the correct answer.

Which of these details is *not* included in the ad?

A ticket prices

B a website for ordering tickets

C a phone number for ordering tickets

D dates that the play will be performed

> ✓ On-the-Boards Children's Theater wants to get readers interested in seeing the play. The ad states two ways to order tickets and the dates of the performances, but you'll have to call or go on the Internet to find out how much they cost. Listing prices might discourage some people from attending. The answer is choice A.

What detail in the ad suggests that your class might want to take a field trip to see the play?

_____

_____

> ✓ The last line of the ad says "Special school rates available." Here is one answer you can infer from the ad:

For a school group, the price of each ticket is lower than it is for people buying one or two tickets at a time.

Test Yourself

Read the passage. Then answer the questions.

The Conscience of John Fairfield

by Frank Maltesi

abolitionist
before the Civil War, a person who sought an immediate end to slavery

If a movie were ever made about John Fairfield, the ads would say, "Based on a true story." "Based on" is as close as anyone can come to the facts of Fairfield's life. Few details are known about him, and some seem to be the stuff of legend, like the tales of King Arthur or Robin Hood. In fact, it is not even certain that John Fairfield was his real name. But true or not, Fairfield's story would make an amazing movie.

John Fairfield was born before 1830 in an area of Virginia that is now part of West Virginia. His father and uncle were Virginia planters who owned slaves. Despite growing up in the slave-holding culture of the South, John in his teens concluded that slavery was wrong. He became a secret abolitionist. An enslaved African American on his uncle's plantation was his best friend. When he was 20, John helped this young man escape to freedom across the Ohio River. When he returned, John learned that his uncle meant to have him arrested. John fled, taking several more of his uncle's slaves with him. He led them north through the Appalachian Mountains and on to Canada.

UNIT 2
Key Ideas and Details

54

"I never saw such a man as Fairfield," a man he had helped escape said years afterward. "He told us he would take us out of slavery or die in the attempt, if we would do our part…. We all agreed to fight till we died rather than be captured."

Fairfield's legend had just begun. He had inherited money, so he could devote himself fully to the abolitionist cause. In Indiana, he met Levi Coffin, a leader of the Underground Railroad. Coffin saw that Fairfield's cleverness and courage would make him an outstanding "conductor." By some accounts, it was Coffin who planned some of Fairfield's daring escapes. But it was Fairfield who pulled them off. He was said to have conducted raids in "nearly every slave state," and to have rescued "thousands" of people from slavery.

Underground Railroad
a secret network of people who helped slaves escape to freedom

On one occasion, Fairfield was asked by some former slaves to help free their relatives, who were enslaved at a salt works in what is now Charleston, West Virginia. Fairfield could pass himself off as a southern gentleman, since after all he was one. He went to Charleston disguised as a businessman from Kentucky. With him were two free African Americans posing as his slaves. He persuaded some local men to invest in a business to build boats to haul salt down the Kanawha River. While he supervised the building of the boats, his "slaves" scouted the area to find their relatives. Under cover of night, they were smuggled on board the boats and escaped down the river. Fairfield pretended to be angry over the loss of his "slaves." He organized a search party, which he sent in the wrong direction while he got away on horseback.

Fairfield used many tricks and disguises. Once he led slaves from Kentucky south into Tennessee to throw slave catchers off their trail. Another time he posed as a funeral director and led a group of slaves to freedom disguised as a funeral procession. He was captured and jailed once in Bracken County, Kentucky, but managed to escape.

Levi Coffin was a Quaker and opposed violence. He was troubled that Fairfield carried guns and armed the slaves he was helping to escape. Fairfield showed him wounds he had received in a fight with slave catchers. "Slaveholders are all devils, and it is no harm to kill the devil," he allegedly told Coffin. "When I undertake to conduct slaves out of bondage, I feel it is my duty to defend them to the last drop of my blood."

allegedly
according to what has been said

Apparently he did. For awhile, Coffin persuaded Fairfield to tone down his activities. He opened a grocery store in Indiana, but after two years he disappeared. In 1856, a white man was reported to have been whipped to death in Tennessee for trying to help a group of slaves escape. It is not known whether this man was John Fairfield, but his name never again appears in the historical record.

1 Fairfield's story began in today's state of ____.

   A Ohio

   B Indiana

   C Virginia

   D West Virginia

2 Fairfield's deeds took place during the ____.

   A 1820s and 1830s

   B 1840s and 1850s

   C early 20th century

   D Civil War of 1861–1865

3 Who was Levi Coffin?

   A Fairfield's best friend

   B an Indiana politician

   C a Virginia slaveowner

   D a leader of the Underground Railroad

4 For the escape from Charleston, Fairfield disguised himself as a ____.

   A slave trader

   B businessman

   C funeral director

   D railroad conductor

5 Why was Fairfield so successful at leading slaves to escape to freedom? Use details from the passage to answer this question.

_____

_____

_____

_____

_____

6 Read this sentence below:

> _He was said to have conducted raids in "nearly every slave state"_
> _and to have rescued "thousands" of people from slavery._

Why does the author put some words in quotation marks?

_____

_____

_____

Main Idea and Summaries

RL.5.2, RI.5.2

Vocabulary
piety
transition

A friend starts to tell you about a great book he just read. Chances are the first question you ask him is, "What's it about?" If your friend has understood the book, he can probably answer in a single sentence.

Everything you read is *about* something. Every book, every chapter, every paragraph has a **main idea.** Identifying that main idea—answering the question "What's it about?"—is one of the most important reading skills. Once you know what you're reading *about,* the details all seem to fall into place. The main ideas of each chapter or section are details that support the main ideas of the book or article. The main ideas of each paragraph are details that support the chapter.

Guided Practice

Read the passage. Then answer the questions.

The Legend of Igo and Ono

by Frank Maltesi

In the mountains of Shasta County, California, are two tiny towns with unusual names. They are called Igo and Ono. Some people say the names are Modoc, the language of American Indians who once lived in these mountains. According to a local legend, the names have a different origin.

The story goes back to the California gold rush of the 1840s and 1850s. People from many parts of the world came to California in those years, hungry for gold. Among them were thousands of immigrants from China. Most of them came from the same province in south China, hoping to escape the crushing poverty of the region. A few returned to China with a fortune in gold, but many stayed in the United States. In the late 1860s, Chinese workers built the first railroad over the California mountains. Many of them later settled in small mountain communities as farmers, miners, or small business owners.

All too frequently, racism would rear its ugly head against the Chinese Americans. Other people resented their presence. The Chinese were beaten up and abused in other ways. Laws were passed to prevent their families from joining them.

rear its ugly head
(idiom)—*appear or be mentioned, said of something unpleasant or unwanted*

Find Igo and Ono in an atlas or on an electronic map. Research how many people live in the towns today.

UNIT 2 ▨▨▨▨▨▨▨▨▨▨▨▨▨▨▨▨▨▨▨▨▨▨▨▨▨▨▨▨▨▨▨▨▨▨▨▨▨▨
Key Ideas and Details

In one community, so the legend goes, a mob of miners and cowboys attacked their Chinese neighbors. They forced them out of their homes with clubs and other weapons. The Chinese are said to have shouted, "I go! I go!" as the mob chased them out of town. This pained cry of people driven from their homes was remembered in the name of the town. The Chinese regrouped and settled in another mountain valley several miles away.

A year or two later, some people in Shasta County grew resentful of the "foreigners" in their midst. Again, they whipped up a mob against the Chinese. But the Chinese had had enough of being pushed around. This time, when the mob tried to force them to leave their homes and shops, they shouted "Oh, no! Oh, no!" They fought back. The Chinese remained, and the town of Ono had its name.

Or so, at least, goes the story. Did it really happen? As with all legends, no one is sure today how much is real and how much is colorful make-believe.

What is this article *mainly* about?

  A   the gold rush in California

  B   separating legend from fact

  C   the Chinese in early California

  D   how two towns got their names

> The passage is "about" all these things in one way or another. But only the second paragraph mentions the gold rush. "The Chinese in California" is a much more general idea than the topic of the article, and so is "separating legend from fact." The article is concerned with one specific legend, of how the two towns got their names. The correct answer is choice D.

Which sentence expresses the main idea of the first paragraph?

A   In the mountains of Shasta County, California, are two tiny towns with unusual names.

B   They are called Igo and Ono.

C   Some people say the names are Modoc, the language of American Indians who once lived in these mountains.

D   According to a local legend, the names have a different origin.

> ✓ In most paragraphs, there is one sentence that carries the main idea of the paragraph. It's called the **topic sentence**. In this paragraph, the first three sentences are details that point to the last sentence. The last sentence tells you that the article will be about how the towns got their names, which is the main idea of the passage. Choice D is the correct answer.

What is the topic sentence of the third paragraph?

_____

_____

> ✓ This paragraph introduces the subject of how the Chinese in early California were sometimes treated. This topic in turn supports the main idea of the article—how the towns got their names. The first sentence states the topic. All the other sentences in the paragraph give details that support or explain it. Your answer should be a restatement of the first sentence. Here is a sample answer:

All too frequently, racism would rear its ugly head against the Chinese Americans.

What is a second main idea in the passage?

_____

_____

> ✓ Many items that you read have a secondary main idea connected to the first. This passage is mainly about how Igo and Ono got their names. But it is also about people choosing to stand up for themselves. Here is one way of stating the answer:

> After being driven out of one community, the Chinese fought back.

Which of these ideas should be left out of a summary of the passage?

A A legend tells how Igo and Ono got their names.

B The names may have come from an American Indian language.

C Chinese immigrants settled in a small mountain town.

D When their second settlement was attacked, the Chinese fought.

> ✓ A **summary** is a short restatement of the ideas in a passage. It should only include the main ideas and the most important supporting details. For this passage, choices A, C, and D are all important details, but a summary need not include that the towns' names may come from an American Indian language. The correct answer is choice B.

Write a summary of the passage.

_____

_____

_____

_____

_____

One way to summarize a well-written passage is to think of the main ideas of each section or paragraph. Here is one possible summary of this passage:

There is a legend about how the towns of Igo and Ono in California got their names. Chinese immigrants settled in one mountain town after the gold rush. When a mob attacked them, they fled the town, crying, "I go!" They started another community nearby. However, when another mob tried to drive them out, they fought back, shouting, "Oh, no!"

Read the passage. Then answer the questions.

The Washerwoman's Donkey

a fable from India

There once was a poor woman who earned her living by taking in laundry. She had a donkey that would carry the dirty laundry down to the river and the clean laundry back to town. The donkey became weak and broken-down from carrying the heavy loads. Finally, one day he refused to carry any more. The woman wanted him to get well, but she was too cheap to buy him hay. She covered him with a tiger's skin to keep him warm and, during the night, brought him to a neighbor's pasture where he could graze.

The donkey soon discovered that the other animals kept their distance from him. He realized that they all thought he was a tiger. So he ate as much as he wanted and soon began feeling strong again.

The farmer who owned the pasture came by. He was alarmed when he saw a tiger among his animals. He wrapped his gray cloak around himself and began to sneak away.

Just then the donkey looked up and saw the gray figure. He thought it was a female donkey. It was love at first sight. Happily, he began hurrying after her. Seeing the tiger bounding toward him, the terrified farmer began to run faster. The donkey was dismayed to see his love flee from him. But he quickly realized that she was only running because she thought he was a tiger. So he gave out a loud bray.

Now the farmer understood that it was no tiger that was after him. He picked up a stick and drove the donkey from his pasture.

What challenge does the donkey face at the beginning of the story?

A He wishes to find a mate.

B Other animals make fun of him.

C He is beaten by the washerwoman.

D He is weak and tired from his work.

This question asks about a detail that supports the main idea of the story. Nowhere does it state that the donkey is looking for a mate, that other animals make fun of him, or that the washerwoman beats him. But she does make him carry heavy loads, which suggests that the correct answer is choice D.

How does the donkey respond to his challenge?

A He disguises himself as a tiger.

B He runs away to a farmer's pasture.

C He refuses to carry anymore loads.

D He lets other animals think he is a tiger.

> This is yet another detail that supports the main idea. The donkey is not clever enough to assume the disguise of a tiger or bold enough to run away or to refuse to work anymore. But when he realizes that other animals think he's a tiger, he sees an advantage for himself. Choice D is the correct answer.

What is the theme of this story?

> The main idea of a literary text is sometimes called its **theme.** The theme is different from the plot or storyline. The plot is "What happens." The theme is "What it's about." In a fable like this, the theme is often expressed as a lesson, or "moral." The lesson often results from the way the main character responds to challenges. The donkey is made a fool of because he pretends to be a tiger. It's his lesson, not the washerwoman's or the farmer's. Here is one possible answer:

Don't pretend to be something you're not.

Which sentence is the *best* summary of paragraph 4?

A The donkey falls in love.

B The farmer runs from the donkey.

C The tiger skin causes comical confusion.

D The donkey shows that he is not a tiger.

> Did you notice that this paragraph does not have a topic sentence? No single sentence expresses the main idea of the paragraph. What happens in it is that both the donkey and the farmer are fooled in ways that create a comical situation like those in TV cartoons. An expression of its main idea should summarize this situation, as choice C does and the other choices do not. Choice C is correct.

Write a summary of the story.

_____

_____

_____

_____

_____

✔ The story is short, so your summary will be even shorter. Your answer should include only the main things that happen in each paragraph. Here is a sample answer:

A washerwoman is too cheap to buy hay for her donkey, so she puts him in a farmer's pasture with a tiger skin on. The donkey finds an advantage in having other animals think he's a tiger. But when the donkey mistakes the farmer for a female donkey, he brays so that she won't be afraid of him. The farmer, no longer fooled, drives him away.

Read the poem. Then answer the questions.

My Heart Leaps Up

by William Wordsworth

My heart leaps up when I behold
    A rainbow in the sky:
So was it when my life began;
So is it now I am a man;
5 So be it when I shall grow old,
    Or let me die!
The Child is father of the Man;
And I could wish my days to be
Bound each to each by natural piety.

piety
religious feeling, or regard for one's parents

What is the main idea that Wordsworth expresses in this poem?

A Rainbows are beautiful.

B Seeing a rainbow makes me feel like a child again.

C I hope I die before I get too old to appreciate nature.

D I hope I never lose the sense of wonder that I had as a child.

> Wordsworth, who lived in England from 1770 to 1850, often wrote about his childlike sense of wonder. Here that sense is expressed in all the answer choices. But which is the main idea, and which are the details that *support* it? Choices A, B, and C all support the theme. The theme itself is expressed by the correct answer choice D.

What does Wordsworth mean by "The Child is father of the Man" in line 7?

_____

_____

> This line is a metaphor for Wordsworth's theme. The key is the last line. *Piety* is a word that means "religious feeling," but 200 years ago, it also meant "regard for one's parents." He feels piety toward his "father," the child who shaped his sense of wonder. One possible answer is:

Wordsworth means that our experiences as children shape who we become as adults.

Test Yourself

Read the passage. Then answer the questions.

Flying Cars: Here at Last

by Al Landsdown

Is it a flying car or a plane you can drive on the highway? Whatever you call it, it's no longer the stuff of science fiction. It's a road machine with wings that unfold for flying. You may see one zooming through traffic—or above it—by 2012.

The new vehicle is called the Transition. It's a product of a Massachusetts company called Terrafugia. That's an Italian word that means, "escape from the ground." It was designed by five former students from the Massachusetts Institute of Technology who are also pilots.

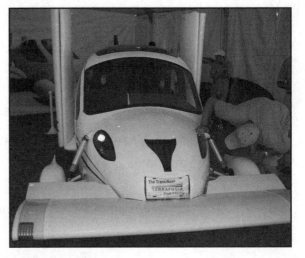

Flying cars have long been a dream of engineers— and technology fans. They were first proposed in 1909, when both cars and planes were new. In the 1950s and 1960s, some models were actually built and tested. They could not be built well or cheaply enough to sell. They did help to inspire an animated TV series, *The Jetsons.* It was about a suburban family in an imagined future that got around in flying cars. The 1982 film *Blade Runner* was a science-fiction thriller in which police of the future patrolled Los Angeles in flying squad cars. But in 1982, cell phones, too, were the stuff of science fiction. And in 1960, no one could have even imagined the Internet.

The Transition is not designed to take off from a street or highway. It needs about half a mile of runway to get airborne. Its builders see it as a private plane that you can drive to the airport. On the highway, it gets about 30 miles per gallon of gas. It takes about a minute to unfold the wings. In the air, it can fly about 400 miles on a tank of gas at a speed of 115 miles per hour. When the trip is over, you don't have to leave the Transition in a hangar. You just fold up the wings, drive home, and park in your garage.

In June 2010, the Transition passed government air and highway safety tests. By then, Terrafugia had already received 70 orders. Don't expect to see many of them around the neighborhood just yet, though. The price tag is $194,000, and that's without a radio or a parachute. For the near future, flying cars will be luxuries for the wealthy, but back in 1909, so were cars.

1 What is the main idea of this article?

   A Flying cars have long been a subject of science fiction.

   B The Transition has wings that fold up for highway use.

   C You can expect to see Transitions soon in your town or city.

   D The first practical flying car is almost ready for road and sky.

2 What is the *most* important supporting idea of this article?

   A The Transition gets better gas mileage than most cars.

   B The Transition is too expensive ever to become popular.

   C Yesterday's science fiction can become today's technology.

   D The first flying cars were actually built more than 50 years ago.

3 Which of these is the topic sentence of the first paragraph?

   A Is it a flying car or a plane you can drive on the highway?

   B Whatever you call it, it's no longer the stuff of science fiction.

   C It's a road machine with wings that unfold for flying.

   D And you may see one zooming through traffic—or above it— by 2012.

4 Which of these would make the *best* heading for paragraph 4?

   A How a Flying Car Works

   B No Need for a Cab to the Airport

   C Your Transition: An Owner's Manual

   D Facts and Figures About the Transition

UNIT 2 ▓▓▓▓▓▓▓▓▓▓▓▓▓▓▓▓▓▓▓▓▓▓▓▓▓▓▓▓
Key Ideas and Details

5 Write a sentence that expresses the main idea of paragraph 3.

_____

_____

_____

_____

_____

6 Write a summary of the article.

_____

_____

_____

_____

_____

Literary Elements

RL.5.3

Vocabulary
martial arts
salmonella
tepid

Think about the last book of fiction that you really enjoyed. What was it you liked most about it? Was it **characters** and how they responded to one another? Maybe it was the **plot,** the sequence of events that happened in the story. Or was it the **setting?** That's the time and location where the story took place.

In a good story, all of these elements interact with one another. The characters and the ways they think, feel, and behave help drive the plot. The setting helps shape the characters and determine the choices they make. Sometimes the setting almost becomes a character in itself. The events of the plot and the way characters respond to them can change the setting.

A story may be realistic fiction, a myth or folktale, a fantasy, or a tale set in historical times. It may even be told in the form of a poem. But whatever kind of story it is, it will have these three literary elements.

Elements of Fiction

Characters make the story real. An author usually describes how characters look, talk, and behave. The "talk" part is called **dialogue.** Sometimes the way a character talks can be as important as what he or she says. In folktales and fantasies, the characters may be magical creatures or have special powers. If they don't seem like real people in some way, it won't be much of a story.

You can learn about characters in stories in several ways:

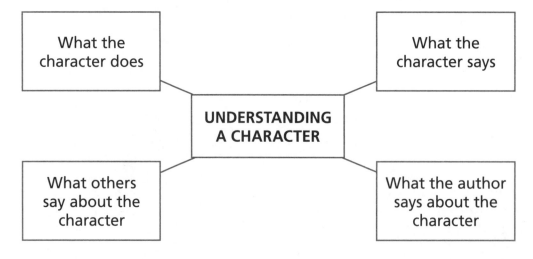

What the character does

What the character says

UNDERSTANDING A CHARACTER

What others say about the character

What the author says about the character

The events of the plot usually take place in chronological (time) order, but they are not always told that way. Part of the story may be told in **flashback,** narrating events that happened earlier. The element of the plot that makes a story exciting is the **conflict.** Sometimes the conflict is a struggle between two or more characters. It may also be an inner conflict, such as a character choosing to do the right thing or not. Or, it may be a conflict between a character and the setting, such as a person struggling to survive in a hostile wilderness or city slum.

Any plot will have an **inciting incident,** which sets the conflict in motion. In "Cinderella," for example, the inciting incident is the announcement of the prince's ball. Most of the plot consists of **rising action,** which continues until you know how the conflict will turn out. That point is called the **climax.** In "Cinderella," the climax comes when the prince fits the glass slipper on Cinderella's foot. The **falling action** is made up of all the events that follow that point and that happen as a result of it. It usually includes a **resolution** explaining what happens to the characters. A resolution may take several chapters to conclude, as in J. R. R. Tolkien's *The Lord of the Rings.* Or, it may be as simple as "And they lived happily ever after," as in "Cinderella."

The **setting** is the time and place in which events of the story take place. The time can be past, present, or future. An author uses the setting to create the **tone,** or feeling of the story. Often the setting is an important part of the story's outcome.

Review the first part of the story "Let Us Give Thanks!" on pages 49 and 50 before reading the next passage, from later in the same story. Use what you learn from *both* parts of the story to answer the questions.

Guided Practice

Read the story. Then answer the questions.

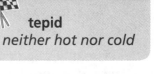

tepid
neither hot nor cold

Let Us Give Thanks!

by Karen Stamfil

"What's holding you up?" Chase said over his shoulder. "It's time to get the bird in the oven."

I poked at the turkey in the sink. The flesh gave—maybe a centimeter. Below the outer layer of skin, it was still frozen solid.

"It needs more time to thaw," I said.

"More time? You've been running hot water over it for an hour!"

"Yeah, Simone," Craig said. He was just coming downstairs, brushing his wet hair. "So that's why there's not enough hot water in the shower."

"Maybe if someone got up just a little bit earlier?" I suggested sweetly. He was right; there was nothing but tepid water coming out of the faucet now.

"And maybe if someone hadn't bought a *frozen* turkey?" Chase said.

"You never said not to," Craig reminded him. "You could have left it on the counter to thaw overnight instead of putting it in the refrigerator."

"Right, and we'd all get salmonella. Real smart, Craig."

Did I detect just the slightest hint of panic in Chase's voice? "Well, that way at least we'd all be together for Thanksgiving," I said. "All of us in the hospital with Dad."

Chase's reply to my witticism was to exhale loudly. He stood there with one hand on his hip, the other holding the big two-tined fork as though ready to fight a duel with the turkey. Mom's She-Who-Must-Be-Obeyed apron barely came down below his beltline, but I didn't think it would be the best moment to laugh about it.

"We need to put it in now," he said decisively. "It'll just take longer to cook."

"Great," Craig deadpanned. "So we'll be able to watch all of the Cowboys' game? I'm glad I bought a lot of snacks."

"What a great idea." Chase was back in control again. "Why don't the two of you go into the living room with Dina and watch TV? Thanks, Simone." He nudged me aside and wrestled the half-frozen bird out of the sink. Greasy water dripped on the floor as he carried it to the counter.

"Somebody ought to clean that up," I said, pointing.

"It'll only get messy again," Chase said. He deposited the turkey noisily on the rack in the roasting pan. "I'm serious. Go watch TV. It's a one-person job now. I just need to season it, and in it goes."

"Okay," I said, feeling marginally more confident that we would eat that evening.

salmonella
a type of bacteria that causes food poisoning

UNIT 2
Key Ideas and Details

Dina was watching the parade from New York. She was still in her pajamas. A woman and a man with breathlessly cheery voices were describing the play-by-play. Just then a float was passing that had all the *Toy Story* characters on it. The woman was describing the enormous, waving Woody and Buzz as if it were the cleverest thing in the world. Watching Chase was more entertaining. But we sat down and watched with Dina until the chef emerged, drying his hands on a towel.

"Well, that's that," he said. "So we'll eat at five instead of four. No harm, no foul."

"Let's hope it isn't no *fowl*," Craig said, his eyes on the TV.

"Very punny, Craig," Chase said. "Simone, your next job will be to baste the turkey every 20 minutes or so. I'm going to take a break."

"What about stuffing?" Dina said. "Mom always makes the best stuffing."

"That's Dad who makes the stuffing," Craig said.

"What about it?" I said. "You going to follow Dad's recipe, or have you got one of your own?"

"Relax, kids," Chase said, settling his long body down on the couch. "This turkey didn't need stuffing. It wasn't empty."

Find a turkey recipe in a cookbook or on the Internet. What mistake is Chase making?

Use information from *both* excerpts to answer the following questions:

Which of these phrases *best* describes Chase as he sees himself?

- **A**   witty and clever
- **B**   smart and capable
- **C**   kind and generous
- **D**   mature and responsible

> Chase may think of himself as all these things. We mainly know about him from what he says and what Simone tells us, so we don't know exactly what he's thinking. But from the confidence with which he takes charge of the Thanksgiving preparations, we can guess that the *main* thing Chase likes to think about himself—at least in this context—is that he has everything under control. That's why choice B is the correct answer.

Which of these phrases *best* describes Chase as Simone sees him?

A a complete fool

B fully ready to be an adult

C a nice but flawed big brother

D someone whose attitude she resents

> We are in Simone's mind in this story. Though she never directly states how she feels about Chase, she reveals her feelings in her observations and her dialogue. She thinks the word *sophomore,* "wise fool," describes him, so choice B wouldn't be right. She is amused by his attitude, as she probably wouldn't be if she resented it (choice D) or thought he was a *complete* fool (choice A). She finds it "entertaining" to watch him cook. She's a loving sister, but she is too wise herself to buy her brother's attitude. Choice C is the correct answer.

How do the plot, the setting, and the character of Chase interact?

_____

_____

_____

_____

_____

_____

> The conflict in this story is between Chase's opinion of himself as a cook and reality. Here is one possible answer:

The suspense in this story centers around the question, "Will Thanksgiving dinner be a complete disaster?" Chase thinks he knows how to cook, but the turkey is going into the oven half-frozen, there's no hot water, the floor is a mess, and Chase has only just started cooking. It's Chase against the kitchen, and so far the kitchen is winning.

How did the end of the first excerpt help you anticipate what happens in the second? What prediction can you make about what will happen in the next part of the story? Explain your reasons.

_____

_____

_____

_____

_____

_____

_____

✓ **Here is one a sample answer:**

The first excerpt ends with Simone saying that Chase's comment, "Some people can even burn water," would live on in family legend. This suggests that some sort of disaster will take place in the kitchen. The second excerpt shows the disaster in the making. It hasn't happened yet, but you can predict that one is coming. The humorous tone of the story tells you that it won't be a real disaster, like food poisoning or the house catching fire. But Chase's dinner will probably be pretty bad.

Elements of Drama

Dramatic literature is written to be performed by actors. Drama has been performed live on stages for more than 2,500 years. In recent times, authors have also written dramas for radio, film, and video performance. Like other forms of narrative, dramatic writing tells a story. It also uses special features that give instructions to directors and performers for making the story come alive.

A **play** is a story that is performed by actors. A play for the stage is usually divided into **acts** and **scenes,** as a book is divided into chapters. A scene is part of the action that takes place in one setting.

Characters take part in the play's action. A list of the characters is called the **cast.** It usually appears at the beginning of the play.

The **setting** is the time and place where the action happens. Sometimes the setting is described in a brief introduction that gives the background information about the characters and events in the play.

Dialogue is the words that characters speak. In a **script,** or printed version of a play, dialogue directly follows the character's name.

Stage directions advise actors how to move and speak. In a script, the characters' names, dialogue, and stage directions are printed in different styles of type so that readers can easily spot which is which.

Props are objects that are used by the characters on a stage, such as a cell phone or a pen. **Scenery** is the backgrounds and larger objects that create the setting of the play. **Lighting** refers to the types of lights used on stage and how bright they are. The props, scenery, and lighting are usually described in the stage directions.

Guided Practice

Read the play. Then answer the questions.

Without Flinching

a one-act play by Sarah Dienstag

> **martial arts**
> *sports based on skills once used in military combat*

CHARACTERS:

Ruth McCallan, 12 years old

Andra McCallan, Ruth's mother

Lucas McCallan, Ruth's father

James Nojima, a martial arts instructor, about 30 years old

A receptionist

Students in the martial arts studio, both adults and school-age

Scene 1

The McCallan family apartment in present-day San Francisco. The stage is divided into two halves, each with separate lighting. At right is the family dining area; at left, Ruth's room. It is not a fancy apartment. The furnishings and props should show that the McCallans are not rich, but they have gone to great lengths to give their daughter everything they think she needs.

Lights come up on the dining area. Andra and Lucas McCallan, Ruth's parents, are in a heated discussion. Their conversation is mimed. We do not hear them, but their movements and gestures leave no doubt that they are angry. The only voice we hear is Ruth's.

RUTH: In kendo, it is considered very bad form to duck an attack to avoid being hit. That's one of the first things you learn. But I did duck, and now I'm about to get clobbered.

As Ruth speaks, lights fade on the living room and come up on her room. A shinai, a bamboo stick used in the Japanese sport of kendo, lies on her bed, and a kendo helmet and armor are on the floor at her feet. Ruth looks despondent, as though she has just lost the thing most dear to her in all the world. She is speaking into a digital recording device.

RUTH: I suppose in kendo, there's some Japanese term for what I did, but there's a plain English word that says it just fine. It's called "lying."

Lights black out on Ruth's bedroom. After a moment they come up on the dining area. Ruth and her parents are sitting around a table, eating.

RUTH: —All I want to know is, can I go to the movies with Shauna and Lucille on Saturday? Shauna's mom can drive.

LUCAS: *(with his mouth full)* You've got the age-group regionals next month. Don't you think you ought to be spending more time practicing your tennis?

ANDRA: And not with Shauna! I know she's your best friend, but you need to be around people who can make you stronger.

RUTH: Mom. Dad. *(She takes a deep breath.)* You know, I was thinking I might just give up tennis for awhile after this tournament. *(She sees her parents freeze and look at each other, but she plows gamely on.)* Maybe try something else?

ANDRA: Ruth, honey, you're too good to throw away the time you've spent on tennis.

RUTH: Right, like I didn't lose in the quarterfinals last time? I've been playing tennis since I was 6. I'm never going to be Serena Williams. I just want to do something else for a while.

LUCAS: Like what? Watching TV? Hanging out at the mall?

RUTH: No! Some other sport, like—like I don't know.

LUCAS: But you're good enough that if you keep at it, you can maybe get a college scholarship—

ANDRA: *(interrupting)* And tennis is such a great social sport! That's how your father and I met, you know.

RUTH: Yes, you've told me that story only a million times—

Lights slowly fade to black as they speak.

ANDRA: Don't be disrespectful, young lady!

RUTH: I'm sorry, I'm sorry. Look, Dad, Mom, this isn't that important. It's only a game that you play with a ball.

LUCAS: You would do better if you practiced more—

ANDRA: If you aren't playing tennis, I can certainly find more chores for you to do at home.

RUTH: *(voice over, as the stage darkens)* That's my parents. They love me, and I know they want only what's best for me. But they plan my life like I'm still in diapers. They chose my summer camps and my Girl Scout troop. They're already telling me what classes I should take in high school. How could I tell them about kendo?

Scene 2

A martial arts studio. The audience is at the rear of the studio, looking upstage toward the front, where there is a large window and a door leading to the street. Pairs of fencers in kendo gear are working out. James Nojima walks among them, observing, now and then giving instructions. A receptionist sits at a desk near the door.

Ruth enters upstage, as if on the street, and stares through the window. She is carrying a tennis racket.

Find out more about kendo—where it comes from, how it is practiced, and what a competition is like. Draw a picture that shows kendo competitors in action.

RUTH: *(voice over)* I learned about kendo from a manga—a Japanese comic book. The mask was so cool, and so was the idea of a sport that had been practiced for hundreds of years by samurai and ninja warriors. There was a kendo studio right by the bus stop near the tennis courts where I had my lessons.

After watching for a while, Ruth opens the door and enters the studio. The receptionist looks up, but Ruth does not approach the desk just yet; she is too entranced by the action.

RECEPTIONIST: Yes? May I help you?

RUTH: No, I'm just—well, yes, thank you, you can. Do you have lessons for beginners?

RECEPTIONIST: Certainly we do. *(She opens a drawer of the desk, takes out some papers, and hands them to Ruth.)* Here is a schedule, and an application form you'll need to have signed by your parents. And a health form. You'll need to have your doctor sign that.

RUTH: Thank you. *(She takes the papers and stares at them.)*

RECEPTIONIST: Is there a problem?

RUTH: *(hesitantly)* N—no. *(with determination)* No, there's no problem.

Which of these sentences *best* describes the interaction between Ruth and her parents?

A   Ruth feels that she never has any fun.

B   Ruth doesn't appreciate how much her parents do for her.

C   Ruth wishes her parents would let her make her own choices.

D   Ruth feels lucky that her parents want her to play tennis instead of doing chores.

✓   You can tell that Ruth's conflict with her parents will lead her to a decision that will land her in trouble. As she sees it, she can't communicate with them about her choices. Her dialogue tells us that she does love and appreciate them (choice B), but she doesn't feel lucky (choice D). You can't conclude that she feels she never has any fun (choice A), but she plainly does feel that tennis is her parents' choice and not hers any longer. The correct answer is choice C.

Which of these lines from scene 2 is an example of dialogue spoken by Ruth?

A   RUTH:

B   Thank you.

C   Is there a problem?

D   *(She takes the papers and stares at them.)*

✓   This question tests your understanding of how to read dramatic literature. You noticed that *italic* print is used for stage directions (choice D), regular print for dialogue (choices B and C), and CAPITALS for the names of characters that tell who is speaking the dialogue (choice A). The play shows you that choice C is the receptionist's line. Choice B is Ruth's line. Choice B is the correct answer.

Read the last line of this excerpt below.

RUTH: *(hesitantly)* N—no. *(with determination)* No, there's no problem.

What do the stage directions in this line tell you?

A   Ruth has just come to a decision.

B   Ruth moves across the stage here.

C   Ruth isn't sure she wants to do kendo.

D   Ruth speaks the line without expression.

> ✓ The stage directions tell the actor playing Ruth how she should speak the line. They tell her that she should speak it *with* specific expressions, so you can rule out choice D. They do not describe stage movement (choice B). "Hesitantly" shows that at first something about the forms troubles her. "With determination" shows that she has made up her mind in spite of it, so choice C isn't right either. The correct answer is choice A.

What is an example of a prop used in this play?

_____

> ✓ A prop is an object that can be picked up and moved by an actor. You wouldn't consider furniture or costumes to be props, but there are several in this excerpt, mostly sports equipment. One possible answer is:

A tennis racket is one example of a prop used in the play.

Contrast the settings of the two scenes in this excerpt. How do they appear to an audience? What do they represent to Ruth?

_____

_____

_____

_____

_____

_____

_____

✓ Here is one possible answer:

The first scene takes place in Ruth's apartment, the second in a martial arts studio. The first setting is familiar to most people. The second is not familiar, so it's more interesting. The first scene is mostly talk, while there is plenty of action going on in the studio. For Ruth, home is the familiar world where her parents are in charge, while the martial arts studio is a place where she will be doing something she has chosen.

There Was an Old Man Who Lived in a Wood

Anonymous, an old English ballad

There was an old man, who lived in a wood,
As you may plainly see;
He said he could do as much work in a day,
As his wife could do in three.

5 With all my heart, the old woman said,
If that you will allow,
Tomorrow you'll stay at home in my stead,
And I'll go drive the plow.

But you must milk the Tidy cow,
10 For fear that she go dry;
And you must feed the little pigs
That are within the sty;

And you must mind the speckled hen,
For fear she lay away;
15 And you must reel the spool of yarn
That I spun yesterday.

The old woman took a staff in her hand,
And went to drive the plow;
The old man took a pail in his hand,
20 And went to milk the cow.

But Tidy hinched, and Tidy flinched,
And Tidy broke his nose,
And Tidy gave him such a blow,
That the blood ran down to his toes!

25 High! Tidy! Ho! Tidy! High!
Tidy! do stand still,
If ever I milk you, Tidy, again,
'Twill be sore against my will!

He went to feed the little pigs,
30 That were within the sty;
He hit his head against the beam,
And he made the blood to fly.

He went to mind the speckled hen,
For fear she'd lay astray;
35 And he forgot the spool of yarn
His wife spun yesterday.

So he swore by the sun, the moon, and the stars,
And the green leaves on the tree,
If his wife didn't do a day's work in her life,
40 She should never be ruled by he.

1 The conflict in this poem arises from the _____.

A man thinking his wife is lazy

B man thinking his wife's work is easy

C woman making a bet with her husband

D woman thinking she is stronger than her husband

2 Choose the phrases that *best* fill both blanks in this sentence:

The man usually works _____ while his wife works _____.

A in the forest…in the fields

B during daylight…at night

C outside all day…inside all day

D in the fields…around the house

3 Compare and contrast what happens to the man when he milks the cow with what happens when he feeds the pigs.

_____

_____

_____

_____

_____

4 The last stanza contains the resolution of the story. Explain what happens.

_____

_____

_____

_____

_____

5 What is similar and what is different between the characters, events, and settings in this poem and in the story, "Let Us Give Thanks"?

_____

_____

_____

_____

_____

Analyzing Events and Concepts

RI.5.3

Vocabulary
condense
debris
missionary
sterilized

Nothing happens all by itself. Thomas Jefferson, Ben Franklin, and the rest of the people who started our country didn't just come up with the idea in 1776. Their ideas about freedom and government came partly from books that had been circulating for nearly 100 years—and had been discussed and argued about by American patriots in countless meetings and letters. You click the shutter of a digital camera and an image appears in the view window. You connect the camera to a computer, click the mouse, and your pictures are stored on the hard drive. But the reasons these simple steps work involve complicated ideas and processes, some of which Leonardo da Vinci would have understood 500 years ago.

People, events, and ideas all relate to and interact with one another. When you read for information, understanding the relationships and influences among them can give you insights about what shaped those people, events, and ideas.

Guided Practice

Read the passage. Then answer the questions.

With an adult's permission, carefully wash an empty ketchup bottle and its lid. Experiment with different kinds of liquids. Which ones flow as described in the article?

A Few Words About Ketchup

by Bryan Hollowell

What foods do you eat with ketchup? It is certainly America's most popular condiment. According to one survey, 96 percent of American households keep ketchup on hand. Certainly no Fourth of July barbecue would be complete without it. Yet ketchup (or "cat-si-up," as it was originally called) isn't American at all. It comes to us from Southeast Asia. It was brought to Europe by traders in the 1600s and from there to colonial America.

This ketchup was not made with tomatoes. Tomatoes were native to Mexico and unknown to the rest of the world until the 1500s. Instead, "cat-si-up" was made from pickled fish. Mushrooms, nuts, and spices were added to give it flavor. The first tomato ketchup may have been made in Canada in the 1700s. In 1801, a recipe for it appeared in an American cookbook for the first time. But few Americans were eating tomatoes then. Common belief had it that they were poisonous! There's a story that in 1820 one grower, Colonel Robert Johnson, proved that people's fears of tomatoes were nonsense by eating a whole basket of them on the steps of a New Jersey courthouse.

As tomatoes became a popular food, tomato ketchup also became popular. Farmers made it from tomatoes that had become too ripe to sell. They sold it in jars at local markets. Making ketchup is hard work, so when Jonas Yerks began bottling and advertising it in 1837, it sold and sold across the country. The ketchup you know was born.

"Shake and shake the ketchup bottle; nothing comes and then a lot'll." Richard Armour wrote this rhyme in 1949. It describes a problem every ketchup eater once knew. Ketchup is a kind of liquid that scientists call *thixotropic*. That means it doesn't flow unless acted upon by an outside force (like your hand, or a knife), and then it can be hard to stop. Another problem with ketchup is that people often eat it with foods that are not very good for them. Around 1990, people were eating fewer burgers and fries due to concern for their health. Ketchup sales fell.

Then in 1991, an inventor named Paul Brown came up with a kind of valve. It fit into the cap of a plastic bottle. Squeezing the bottle made the ketchup flow easily. When you stopped squeezing, air sucked the ketchup back in, and the valve closed. Brown's valves are used in shampoo bottles (another thixotropic liquid) and in babies' sippy cups. It was the ketchup makers, however, who made him rich. Soon they were selling ketchup in enormous bottles. They were displayed upside down on store shelves. Ketchup sales soared.

How did ketchup get to America?

- **A** American Indians discovered it.
- **B** Colonists brought it from Europe.
- **C** Immigrants brought it from Asia.
- **D** Christopher Columbus introduced it.

This is a detail you can find directly in the text. "Cat-si-up" indeed came from Southeast Asia. However, it wasn't brought here by Asian immigrants— or by the traders who brought it from Asia to Europe, or by Columbus. It came to America only with the colonists. Choice B is correct.

According to the article, which of these events happened *first?*

A   Tomato ketchup was made in Canada.

B   Tomatoes were proven not to be poisonous.

C   Ketchup recipes appeared in American cookbooks.

D   Tomato ketchup was bottled and sold commercially.

> A chronological **sequence** of events can be important in understanding their relationship. If event X came after event Y, it stands to reason that it couldn't have caused or influenced event Y. Read the details, and you'll see that choice A is the correct answer.

How can you tell that many people before 1820 knew that tomatoes were not poisonous?

_____

_____

_____

_____

> This question may take some thinking. It's a question in which you need to **draw a conclusion** from details in the article and from what you already know. Note the date of Colonel Johnson's demonstration and some of the other dates. One answer might be:

Colonel Johnson proved tomatoes weren't poisonous in 1820, but
a recipe for tomato ketchup was published in a cookbook in 1801.
The Canadians were making it even earlier. You can conclude that it
didn't kill anyone.

The author suggests that ketchup sales "soared" in the 1990s because of the valve Paul Brown invented. Do you think that reason is convincing? Explain why, or why not.

_____

_____

_____

✓ There is no right or wrong answer to this question. You need to ask yourself, "Do the details in the article and what I know support the author's point?" Here is one possible answer:

> No, because I don't believe that it's being hard to get just the right amount of ketchup out of a bottle would stop people from eating it. Richard Armour's rhyme proves that it didn't.

Read the passage. Then answer the questions.

Classic Tomato Ketchup

15–17 medium-sized tomatoes, sliced

$\frac{3}{4}$ cup chopped onions

1 cup cider vinegar

3 inches cinnamon stick

1 teaspoon whole cloves

1 clove garlic, finely chopped

$\frac{1}{2}$ cup sugar, or to taste

$1\frac{1}{4}$ teaspoons salt

1 teaspoon paprika

$\frac{1}{8}$ teaspoon cayenne pepper, or to taste

1. In a large pot, simmer tomatoes and onions together for 20–30 minutes. When cooked, run through a strainer.

2. Place the vinegar in an enamel pan. Add a cloth spice bag containing the cinnamon, cloves, and garlic. Simmer for 30 minutes, then remove the spices.

3. Boil the tomato and onion mixture until reduced to one-half the original volume, stirring frequently. Add the spiced vinegar, sugar, salt, paprika, and cayenne pepper. Bring to a boil again, then boil rapidly for 10 minutes or until the mixture starts to thicken.

4. Pour into clean, hot, sterilized jars. Leave about $\frac{1}{4}$-inch empty space on top. Seal jars tightly and boil in water for five minutes.

5. Cool and serve.

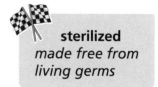
sterilized
made free from living germs

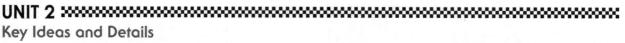

Which of these steps do you do *first?*

A   Let it cool.

B   Add the sugar.

C   Boil to reduce the volume.

D   Simmer the spices in vinegar.

> Cooking is a process that involves following steps. Each step has a relationship to the next. If you miss a step or do them out of order, you could end up with a bad-tasting mess. Read the recipe carefully, and you'll see that choices A, B, and C are all steps that come *after* simmering the spices in vinegar. Choice D is the correct answer.

Which steps in this recipe can you do at the same time?

A   steps 1 and 2

B   steps 2 and 3

C   steps 3 and 4

D   steps 4 and 5

> This question involves making an inference. Cooks have to follow steps, but they also like to save time. While tomatoes and onions are simmering on one burner, vinegar and spices can be simmering on another. You can't say that about any of the other choices. They all involve steps that can't be done until the previous step is concluded. Choice A is correct. Did you notice that you can also clean and sterilize the jars while doing step 3?

What could happen if you didn't boil the jars after sealing them?

_____

_____

_____

_____

✓ This question asks you to **make a prediction.** You know that boiling the mixture and sterilizing the jars has the purpose of killing harmful bacteria. You can infer that germs may also drop into the ketchup while you're putting it into the jars. Here is one possible answer:

> You can predict that the ketchup you worked so hard to make might not be safe to eat if you didn't sterilize it again, since germs might have dropped into the jars while you were spooning in the ketchup.

Considering *both* this recipe and the article by Bryan Hollowell, where do you think farmers got the idea for making ketchup from tomatoes that were too ripe to sell?

_____

_____

✓ This question asks you to think about the process described in the recipe and combine it with something you know to explain a detail in the article. Does the recipe remind you of anything else you've seen people do in the kitchen, or read about? Does the idea of making ketchup from overripe tomatoes? That's exactly how people preserve fruit to make jam. Here is a possible answer:

> Farmers got the idea from making jam out of fruit that got too ripe.

> **missionary**
> *a person sent to do work on behalf of a religion*

Hard Traveling

by Harry Thelen

In 1842, two men crossed America in opposite directions. They never met, but together they helped add the Pacific Northwest region to the United States.

John Charles Frémont was a 29-year-old lieutenant in the United States Army. He was on a scouting mission to the West. With a well-supplied party of soldiers and guides, Frémont started out in May along the Oregon Trail. This was an old fur-trader's path that since 1836 had become a route west for settlers in covered wagons. Frémont explored passes in the Rocky Mountains. He climbed a mountain in Wyoming that he named for himself. When he returned on October 29, he was convinced that the far West had to become part of the United States. With the help of his talented young wife, Jessie, he wrote a book about his adventures and his idea that the country should expand westward. It became a best seller.

Dr. Marcus Whitman, 40, was a missionary at a tiny settlement he and *his* young wife, Narcissa, had started near today's Walla Walla, Washington. Six years earlier, the Whitmans had been part of the very first wagon train to travel west on the Oregon Trail. They ran a school for American Indian children and also sought to convert the American Indians to Christianity. In 1842, Whitman and the few other American settlers in the region heard some disturbing news. A British trading company was about to claim the whole of the Oregon Territory, which included today's states of Washington and Oregon, part of Idaho, western Montana and Wyoming, and much of western Canada.

> Research the 1842 journeys of John Charles Frémont and Marcus Whitman. Trace their routes on a map of the United States.

Whitman had planned to go east in the spring to persuade his church not to close his mission. Now he took it upon himself to persuade the government to "keep Oregon American." He started on October 3—very late in the year for a Rocky Mountain crossing. He headed south to Santa Fe, which was then part of Mexico. He ran into heavy snow in the mountains and swam his horse through broken ice in Colorado's Grand River. From Santa Fe he headed east. He reached Washington, D.C., in March 1843 after a 3,500-mile journey. He met with President John Tyler and Secretary of State Daniel Webster. Then Whitman went to New York and told his story to a newspaper. In the spring, Whitman headed back to his mission. He found himself part of the biggest wagon train that had ever followed the Oregon Trail.

Many Americans were ready to go to war over Oregon. It was an issue in the 1844 campaign for president. But two years later, a treaty divided the territory peacefully between Britain and the United States.

Which of these events happened *first?*

A Frémont and his wife wrote a book.

B Whitman and his wife opened a mission.

C Frémont scouted passes in the Rocky Mountains.

D Whitman crossed the Rocky Mountains in winter.

> This article organizes events by topic, not in chronological order. You have to read the details to infer that the Whitmans opened their mission in 1836. The events in choices A, C, and D all happened six years later, in 1842 or afterward. The correct answer is choice B.

Why was Marcus Whitman planning to head east in 1843?

_____

_____

> This question asks you to find a reason something happened—to identify **cause and effect.** The effect was that Whitman planned to go east. A detail in the passage identifies the cause. Here is a sample answer:

His church was planning to close his mission, and he was going east to persuade them not to.

UNIT 2 ▓▓▓
Key Ideas and Details

Why did Whitman leave in October 1842 instead?

A He wanted to talk to government leaders about Oregon.

B He wanted to explore new territory for the United States.

C He wanted to guide settlers to Oregon the following spring.

D He wanted to talk to Frémont about his scouting expedition.

> Here again, you're asked to identify a cause. The effect was that Whitman thought the trip was urgent enough that he made a winter crossing of the Rocky Mountains. He had heard that a foreign country was planning to seize Oregon. He met with the president and the secretary of state. He did not meet Frémont. There is no suggestion that he wanted to guide settlers west. By putting these details, you can conclude that his urgent reason was to persuade the government not to let the British seize Oregon. Choice A is the correct answer.

According to the article, how did Frémont's and Whitman's journeys help make the Pacific Northwest part of the United States?

_____

_____

_____

_____

_____

> Here you need to consider the whole article to answer the question. Did Frémont and Whitman directly persuade the government to settle Oregon? How and when did the U.S. get the Oregon Territory? What effect did the Frémonts' book have? What about the story Whitman told the New York newspaper? How did people, events, and ideas interact with one another? Here is one possible answer:

Frémont's journey, as described by his wife in her best-selling book, inspired Americans to go west. Whitman's journey, as reported in the New York newspaper, made going to Oregon seem like a patriotic thing to do. The next spring, a record number of settlers made the journey.

Tornado!

by Einar F. Klamst

condense
to make denser or more compact

It's a hot, humid afternoon on the Great Plains. Thunderstorms are forecast. The gray sky turns a darker, almost greenish shade. The mass of clouds looks like a wall. Large hail begins to fall. Residents of the region know that sky well. It's time to take shelter. It's tornado weather.

A tornado is a violently rotating column of air in contact with the earth. Tornados occur in many parts of the world but most frequently in the central United States in spring and summer. A tornado forms when a layer of warm, moist air is trapped under a layer of cold, dry air. In the early spring, cold air rushing in from the Rocky Mountains causes the warm air layer to be pushed up. As it meets the cold air above it, clouds form and thunderstorms develop in a layer of low pressure. Water vapor in the rapidly rising air condenses in the colder air. Under the right (or wrong) conditions, it begins to rotate around the low-pressure layer. The rising air within the storm tilts the rotating air from horizontal to vertical, forming the well-known funnel-shaped cloud. If it touches the ground—tornado!

In late spring and summer, tornados can start in a different way, along what meteorologists call a "dryline." This is an invisible line with warm, moist air to the east and hot, dry air to the west. During the afternoon, the hot air moves in and pushes the warm, moist air upward. Something similar can happen when the moving hot air flows "uphill," toward higher ground. When the rising moist air meets the cold air above it, thunderstorms develop, and under the right conditions, a tornado.

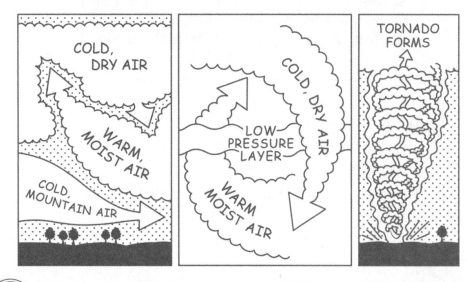

COLD, DRY AIR

WARM, MOIST AIR

COLD, MOUNTAIN AIR

COLD, DRY AIR

LOW-PRESSURE LAYER

WARM MOIST AIR

TORNADO FORMS

Many funnel clouds form without anyone seeing them. They're transparent, because they consist of water vapor. When they touch down, they pick up dust and dirt and become visible. An ordinary tornado has wind speeds of "only" 112 miles per hour and is about 250 feet wide. It travels about a mile before changes in pressure cause it to break up. Only about one tornado in 50 is classified as violent. These can whirl around at speeds greater than 250 miles per hour and exceed two miles in width. They can last more than an hour and carve a path of destruction dozens of miles long.

Most deaths from tornados result from flying debris. When you see the warning signs, take shelter! If no underground shelter is available, stay in an inner room under a sturdy piece of furniture. Stay away from windows. Do you hear a loud roaring sound, like a freight train? A tornado is on its way.

debris
pieces of an object that has been broken down or destroyed

1 Which of these is the *last* warning sign of a tornado?

   A large hail

   B a greenish sky

   C a cloud mass like a wall

   D a roar like a freight train

2 In order for a tornado to form, there must *first* be ____.

   A an area of low pressure

   B cold air rushing in from the west

   C hot, dry air rushing in from the west

   D a layer of warm, moist air under a layer of cold, dry air

3 Because funnel clouds are made up of water vapor, they ____.

   A usually form in cold weather

   B usually form in rapidly rising air

   C are invisible until they touch ground

   D pick up dust and dirt when they touch ground

4 What causes the funnel cloud to form?

_____

_____

_____

_____

_____

5 On the central plains, how does a tornado in early spring form differently than a tornado in summer?

_____

_____

_____

_____

_____

UNIT 2
Key Ideas and Details

REVIEW

Key Ideas and Details

Vocabulary
democracy

Read the passage. Then answer the questions.

Justice

a tale from Ethiopia

In a village like any other, a woman kept a herd of goats. One morning, she noticed that some of her goats had wandered off. She went looking for them in the fields and forests, but she could not find them. Finally, she came upon a man who was brewing coffee alongside the road. "Have you seen any stray goats?" she asked him.

Now, the man had gone deaf years before and couldn't hear a word she said. He thought she was asking how to get to the river. He pointed in the right direction, and the woman thanked him.

The woman found her missing goats grazing peacefully by the river. But a kid had caught its foot between two rocks and broken its leg. Taking the injured animal in her arms, she began to guide the rest of the goats homeward. When she came to the road, the man was still there, drinking his coffee.

"Thank you for showing me the way," she said. "A lot of people would have lied, and kept the goats. I'd like you to have this kid in exchange for your kindness."

The man could not hear her. He thought she was blaming him for the animal's broken leg. "How could you think I had anything to do with that?" he said angrily.

"But you pointed to the river!" the woman said, bewildered. "The goats were right where you said they would be!"

"I never saw this goat before in my life!" the man shouted. "Go away and leave me in peace!"

By this time, a number of people had happened along. As people will, they stopped to listen to the argument. "I wanted to give this man a goat because he helped me," the woman complained to them, "and all he does is yell at me!"

"Liar!" the man yelled at her. "I do not mistreat animals! Goats are always breaking bones!" He waved his arm and accidentally struck the woman with the back of his hand.

"Oh!" the woman cried, more from indignation than injury. "Did you see that? I'm going to take him before the wise judge who lives in the next village!"

"Accusing me of harming her goat!" the man roared. "She has damaged my reputation! For that, I must take her before the judge!"

Followed by a great crowd of people, the woman and the man walked to the neighboring village, hurling accusations at each other the entire way. When they reached the village, they called for the wise judge to come out and give justice.

The crowd fell silent as the judge came out of his house. He sat on a stool, nodding sagely as first the man, then the woman, gave their explanations of what had happened. Then the people in the crowd eagerly began to tell their versions of the story. But to the judge, it was all without meaning, for he was as deaf as the man who stood before him. He thought that the man and woman were husband and wife. Also, if the truth were known, he couldn't see very well either. He thought that the goat in the woman's arms was their baby.

At last, the judge held up his hand, and the crowd quieted down. "It is not good for families to quarrel," he said to the man. "It creates disharmony in the village. You should be ashamed of yourself. From this time forward, be kind to your wife."

Then he turned to the woman. "As for you," he said, "such laziness is unseemly. From now on, be on time with your husband's dinner."

The judge squinted at the kid in the woman's arms. He thought it was the most beautiful baby he had ever seen. "May your child have a long and happy life," he said. "May she bring joy to your family and honor to your village."

The judge went back into his house to take a nap. The man and woman went their separate ways, shaking their heads. The crowd began to scatter.

"Oh, how wise he is!" one woman said.

"Yes," a man agreed. "How did we ever get along before we had justice?"

UNIT 2 :::
Key Ideas and Details

1 Which of these *best* states the theme of this story?

   A Justice is blind.

   B It all depends on your point of view.

   C The wise are not always as wise as people think.

   D Don't ask anyone else to solve your problems for you.

2 This story comes from Ethiopia, which is a country in _____.

   A Asia

   B Africa

   C Europe

   D Central America

3 Which of these is the topic sentence of paragraph 3?

   A The woman found her missing goats grazing peacefully by the river.

   B But a kid had caught its foot between two rocks and broken its leg.

   C Taking the injured animal in her arms, she began to guide the rest of the goats homeward.

   D When she came to the road, the man was still there, drinking his coffee.

4 Why did the woman take the man before the judge?

   A He hit her.

   B He yelled at her.

   C He hurt her goat.

   D He accused her of lying.

5 The judge lived in _____.

   A a nearby city

   B the man's village

   C the woman's village

   D a different village than either of them

6 What is the main idea of paragraph 13?

    A Everyone respected the judge's decisions.

    B The judge listened to everyone's explanation.

    C The judge could not hear and was almost blind.

    D The judge thought that the goat was the woman's baby.

7 Which of these details does *not* belong in a summary of the story?

    A The man was making coffee beside the road.

    B The man and woman took their case to a judge.

    C A woman went looking for some missing goats.

    D The man thought the woman was accusing her of hurting the goat.

8 We know that the judge is wise *mainly* because of what _____.

    A he says

    B he does

    C the narrator tells us

    D the other characters tell us

9 Who in this story gets "justice"? Explain why.

_____

_____

_____

_____

_____

UNIT 2 ▨▨▨▨▨▨▨▨▨▨▨▨▨▨▨▨▨▨▨▨▨▨▨▨▨▨▨▨▨▨▨▨▨▨
Key Ideas and Details

The Vote

by Amanda Williams

It happened in November 1805, and it happened far from the United States. Yet some have called it one of the most important elections in American history.

It took place in present-day Washington State, on the north bank of the Columbia River near the Pacific Ocean. The famous Lewis and Clark expedition had reached this campsite days earlier. It was 18 months since they had left St. Louis, Missouri, to explore the unknown West. In the spring, they would start back to report their findings to President Thomas Jefferson. But for now, they had an urgent question. Where in this wet, green wilderness should they spend the winter? Should they stay where they were, cross to the south bank of the river, or go back upriver to get a head start on next spring's journey home?

The expedition's survival could depend on their decision. To make it through the winter, they would need water, food, and shelter. Their supply of goods for trade with the Indians was almost gone, so they would have to hunt for their meat. Captain Meriwether Lewis argued for the south bank. The winter would be harsher upriver, and they would have to wait for snow in the mountains to melt before they could start home anyway. The south bank had easier trails to the ocean, where men could be put to work making salt. All the men, Lewis said, craved salt. There was a chance, too, that a trading ship might arrive.

Captain William Clark didn't care about salt. But he, too, favored the south bank. The Clatsop Indians had told him that there were elk there, while to the north were mostly deer. Elk were bigger, easier to shoot, and their skins made better clothing.

Both the captains agreed. Nevertheless, they decided to put the decision to a vote.

Why was this important? The Lewis and Clark expedition was a military operation. The two leaders were captains in the United States Army. The men—all but two—were soldiers under their command. The army was not a democracy. Discipline was kept through order and obedience. Still, they let the men vote on the crucial question of where to spend the winter.

Not only the men, though. With them was Sacagawea, the young Shoshone woman who had been their guide during this second year of the expedition. It was thanks to her that they had found their way through the Rocky Mountains and that they had obtained the promise of Indian horses for the return trip. Back in the United States, American Indians did not vote in elections, and women would not win the right to vote for more than 100 years. But Sacagawea got a vote in this election, same as the soldiers.

So did York. He was an African American and Clark's personal slave. Back in the States, most African Americans were enslaved, and even free black men couldn't vote in most states. However, York voted in this election.

The Lewis and Clark expedition made it back to St. Louis in September 1806. It had been an amazing achievement. It had mapped new territory, made notes on dozens of native tribes, and recorded lists of words in Indian languages. It had catalogued more than 200 plants and animals that were previously unknown to science. It had lost only one man, to disease. In a small but significant way, it had advanced the progress of democracy.

The result of the vote? It was almost unanimous in favor of the south bank.

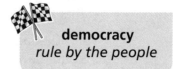

democracy
rule by the people

10 According to the author, why was this an important election?

_____

_____

_____

_____

_____

UNIT 2 ▨▨▨▨▨▨▨▨▨▨▨▨▨▨▨▨▨▨▨▨▨▨▨▨▨▨▨▨▨▨▨▨▨▨▨▨▨
Key Ideas and Details

11 Besides the vote, what is the *next* important point the author makes?

   A Most African Americans were then enslaved.

   B Lewis and Clark were brave and wise commanders.

   C Sacagawea guided the expedition during its second year.

   D The Lewis and Clark expedition was an amazing achievement.

12 Which of these is the topic sentence of paragraph 2?

   A Where in this wet, green wilderness should they spend the winter?

   B The famous Lewis and Clark expedition had reached this campsite days earlier.

   C It was 18 months since they had left St. Louis, Missouri, to explore the unknown West.

   D In the spring, they would start back to report their findings to President Thomas Jefferson.

13 The vote took place in what is today the state of _____.

   A Oregon

   B Virginia

   C Missouri

   D Washington

14 What was the *main* reason Lewis hoped a trading ship would arrive?

   A It would have supplies to sell them.

   B It would be able to take them home.

   C The sailors would be good company for the men.

   D It could bring news of the expedition to the States.

15 Lewis and Clark put the vote to the men _____.

   A after they had started back upriver

   B after they had discussed the question

   C before they reached the Pacific Ocean

   D before they learned about the country from the Clatsops

16 Based on the article, which of these was *not* one of the goals of the Lewis and Clark expedition?

    A to reach the Pacific Ocean

    B to claim new territory for the United States

    C to make friendly contact with American Indians

    D to record plants and animals unknown to science

17 You can predict that when the expedition started back in the spring, ____.

    A they were eating their meat without salt

    B Clark had made up his mind to set York free

    C they had plenty of goods to trade with the Indians

    D most of the men were wearing clothes made of elk skin

18 Write a summary of the passage. Include only the main ideas and most important details.

_____

_____

_____

_____

_____

UNIT 2
Key Ideas and Details

Craft and Structure

Writing is more than putting down words on paper. There's a craft to it, much as there is to building furniture. A writer carefully considers the language he uses, thinking about his purpose and his audience. She puts together sentences, paragraphs, and longer sections such as chapters in ways that help move a story or an article forward or that help the reader better understand the information she is presenting. Any writer has a point of view and reasons for writing and will craft his sentences and paragraphs to advance them.

This unit is about the ways that writers craft and structure their work, and their reasons for doing it. As you read, it's important to recognize this craft and structure, just as you can recognize in the work of a furniture builder that some pieces are plain and others fancy, and that a bed is designed for sleeping and a cabinet for putting things in.

● **In Lesson 8,** you'll learn about craft and structure in a literary text—how paragraphs and chapters, stanzas and scenes fit together to tell a story or show how a character grows and learns, and how an author uses structure to keep you turning the pages.

● **Lesson 9** is about craft and structure in informational text. You'll learn about the different ways that writers structure their work to present information, and how the structure they choose depends on the kind of information they want you to know.

● **Lesson 10** is about point of view in both literary and informational texts. You'll learn how the point of view of an author or a character influences the way events in a story are described, and how your own point of view can shape the way you read and understand them. In informational text, you'll learn how to recognize the author's purpose for writing, and how that purpose reflects the author's point of view.

Literary Structure

RL.5.5

Vocabulary
air
fret
melancholy
reel
visage

A book is divided into chapters, a play into acts and scenes, and a poem into stanzas. These divisions are not just a convenient way to break your reading into bite-sized chunks. A well-crafted series of chapters, scenes, or stanzas build on one another. The author wants you to read on to find out what happens next. Even in a poem that expresses feelings without telling a story, the ideas and images build on one another in a sequential way to support the theme. Within a chapter, even within a paragraph, the individual sentences can fit together to provide structure. It adds to your enjoyment and understanding of literature when you can recognize these structural elements.

Guided Practice

Read the song. Then answer the questions.

The Arkansas Traveler

an American popular song of the 1850s

Oh, once upon a time in Arkansas,
An old man sat in his little cabin door
And fiddled at a tune that he liked to hear,
A jolly old tune that he played by ear.
It was raining hard, but the fiddler didn't care,
He sawed away at the popular air[1]
Though his roof tree leaked like a water fall,
That didn't seem to bother the man at all.

A traveler was riding by that day,
And stopped to hear him practicing away.
The cabin was afloat and his feet were wet,
But still the old man didn't seem to fret.[2]
So the stranger said, "Now, the way it seems to me,
You'd better mend your roof," said he.
But the old man said, as he played away,
"I couldn't mend it now, it's a rainy day."

---

[1]**air:** song

[2]**fret:** worry

The traveler replied, "That's all quite true,
But this, I think, is the thing for you to do:
Get busy on a day that is fair and bright,
Then pitch the old roof till it's good and tight."
But the old man kept on playing at his reel,[3]
And tapped the ground with his leathery heel.
"Get along," said he, "for you give me a pain!
My cabin never leaks when it doesn't rain!"

Summarize what happens in each stanza of this song.

Stanza 1 _____

_____

Stanza 2 _____

_____

Stanza 3 _____

_____

    Did you notice how each stanza, or verse, of this song is like a chapter in a longer literary work? Each has a main idea. The first stanza establishes the setting and introduces the conflict. The second stanza brings in a second character, the traveler, who attempts to resolve the problem. In the third stanza, the traveler makes another attempt to resolve it, but the old man does so himself—in a comical way that seems to say, "what problem?" Your answer should address the structure of the song in this way but be more specific about what happens. Here is a sample answer:

Stanza 1—A man is fiddling in front of his cabin while rain pours through his leaky roof.

Stanza 2—A traveler advises the old man to fix his roof. The old man says he can't do it because it's raining.

Stanza 3—The traveler suggests that he fix it after the rain stops. The old man replies that his cabin doesn't leak when it isn't raining.

[3]reel: dance

The structure of this song *most* resembles a ____.

A play

B joke

C fable

D mystery

With a group, use the Internet to find out more about American popular songs of the 1800s. Choose a song and do a presentation for your class about it.

Have you ever noticed that a lot of jokes are little stories? They have a setting, characters, and a conflict that ends in a climax—the "punch line," in which the conflict is "resolved" in a way that makes you laugh. This song (which came from a play of the same title) is structured like that, rather than like a play, a fable, or a mystery. There is no character development, no moral, no suspense; only a laugh at the end. The correct answer is choice B.

Review the first two scenes of the play "Without Flinching" on pages 76–78 before reading the next part of the play. Use what you learn from both parts of the play to answer the questions.

Guided Practice

Read the play. Then answer the questions.

Use the library or the Internet to find a glossary of the Japanese terms used in kendo. What is the meaning of *yame, men tore,* and the other terms you read in scene 3?

Without Flinching

Scene 3

The martial arts studio. The stage is dark at first, with lights gradually brightening during Ruth's voice-over to reveal pairs of fencers practicing as in the previous scene, with James Nojima walking among them and observing. Ruth is among them, center stage, clearly outmatched by another girl.

RUTH: *(voice-over)* The ritual of kendo grabbed me from the first day. There's an exact right way to do everything, like folding your uniform and taking care of your gear, even sitting on the floor at the beginning of each practice session. You sit in order of rank, so as a lowly six-*kyu* beginner I was in the back row. But that was cool. There's a lot of Japanese terms that you have to learn, and gestures of respect for the coach. We call him *sensei,* which means "teacher," and it's a term of great respect, whether you're talking about a university professor or the playground supervisor at a preschool.

JAMES: *(shouting in Japanese)* Yame! *(pause)* Men tore!

At the first command, the fencers stop. At the second, they take off their helmets, and we see that the girl who has been getting whacked around is Ruth. There is notable relief among the fencers at being given a break.

JAMES: *(in a normal, conversational voice)* Chakuza, kudasai.

Everyone assumes a formal seated position on the floor facing the fencing area. Ruth starts to join them.

JAMES: *(in English, with no accent)* Not you, Ruth-san. Practice with me, please.

RUTH: Yes—hai, James sensei.

They face each other. By now the other class members are seated on the floor, watching them intently.

JAMES: You must overcome the natural reaction to flinch, Ruth-san. It takes you out of position for a counterattack.

RUTH: Hai, James sensei.

JAMES: You need to cultivate a nonflinching spirit. You want your opponent to strike the air, not you, but you want to be in a position to strike back. You're not going to get hurt. That's what your helmet and protective gear are for.

RUTH: Right.

JAMES: Now then, men tsuke. *(He puts his helmet on and gestures to Ruth, who puts on hers.)* Chudan.

He raises his bamboo sword, and so does she. They hold them crossed above their heads.

JAMES: *(suddenly shouting in Japanese)* Men!

He brings his stick down suddenly to strike Ruth on the top of her helmet, but she backs away.

JAMES: *(with mock sternness)* You flinched again, Ruth-san.

RUTH: *(embarrassed)* Sorry—gomen! *(She takes off her helmet.)* It's hard sometimes even to look at you without flinching, James-sensei!

JAMES: You've learned a lot in two months. Your footwork is good, and you have good reflexes.

RUTH: Thank you. That's from six years of tennis.

JAMES: Yes, I've noticed you always bring a racket with you.

RUTH: *(avoiding his gaze)* Well, yes, there's the tennis club around the corner…

JAMES: You don't flinch when a ball is hit right at you, do you?

RUTH: *(enjoying his attention and his encouragement)* No.

JAMES: Well then, there you are. *(Again he puts on his helmet and gestures to Ruth.)* Again. This time, you attack and I'll defend.

RUTH: Okay—I mean hai!

They assume the position again.

JAMES: Men!

She brings her stick down suddenly, but he steps back neatly and parries the blow with his stick. Sound of blows being struck and shouts in Japanese as lights fade to black.

RUTH: *(voice-over)* His real name is James Nojima, and he's a four-dan kendoka, which is like a super black belt. When he's not being a samurai warrior, he teaches math at a community college. I wish he were my *math* teacher. I bet he could get me to understand algebra.

The stage is almost dark. Ruth dashes across the stage, carrying a gym bag, her tennis racket, and a long cardboard mailing tube.

RUTH: *(voice-over)* The rituals of kendo are supposed to teach you discipline, focus, and honor. I was getting the discipline and focus okay, but not the honor part. The funny thing was, I'm sure Mom and Dad would have been cool with my doing kendo if I talked to them reasonably about it. But just then it seemed important to keep it a secret, something that was all my own.

Scene 4

The apartment. Lights come up on Ruth's room. She is sitting on her bed, scraping slivers from her bamboo sword with sandpaper. The cardboard tube and her gym bag are on the floor beside her, as is her tennis racket and a school backpack.

Ruth looks up in alarm. She quickly shoves the bamboo sword into the tube, pauses to give it a hasty bow, then gets up and stuffs the tube and her gym bag into the back of her closet.

ANDRA: *(offstage)* Ruth? Ruth, honey?

UNIT 3 ▨▧▨▧▨▧▨▧▨▧▨▧▨▧▨▧▨▧▨▧▨▧▨▧▨▧▨▧▨▧▨▧▨▧▨
Craft and Structure

RUTH: In my room, Mom.

Now Ruth notices the piece of sandpaper. She grabs it, looks around, and stuffs it under her pillow, just as lights come up on the dining room. Andra, dressed for work, crosses the stage toward Ruth's room. Ruth barely has time to grab the tennis racket. She is sitting on the bed, holding it, just as Andra reaches her door. Her mother knocks but opens the door before Ruth says…

RUTH: Come in.

What is the *most* important thing the author wants you to know from the beginning of the play?

   A   Ruth is in some sort of trouble.

   B   Ruth disobeys her parents often.

   C   Ruth has played tennis all her life.

   D   Ruth's family doesn't have much money.

> When you first meet Ruth, before you know anything about her or her family, you know she's in trouble. Her parents are arguing, she tells you she's about to get "clobbered," and she hints that it has something to do with lying. The other answer choices may or may not be true statements, but you can predict from that first page of scene 1 that the play is about how Ruth got into trouble—and whether she's going to get out of it. Choice A is the correct answer.

How do the first two scenes reveal the conflict in the play?

_____

_____

> In the first scene, you learn that Ruth is in trouble, and that she is active in the Japanese sport of kendo. You see that her parents find it very important that she plays tennis, that she's getting tired of it, and that (at least as Ruth sees it), her parents don't listen to her. In the second scene, you see how Ruth got started with kendo. There are application forms involved, and that bothers Ruth—for a second or two. That action suggests the conflict, and why Ruth is in trouble with her parents. Here is one possible answer:

The conflict is that Ruth has been doing kendo without her parents'
knowledge or permission. Now her deception has been found out.

How does the conflict build in scenes 3 and 4?

_____

_____

_____

_____

_____

✓ **Here is one possible answer:**

    In scene 3, you see that Ruth has really come to love kendo and enjoy her relationship with her instructor, James. Her words and actions in scene 4 make it clear that it's something she's hiding from her parents. But what about that application form they were supposed to have signed? You can predict that it will hurt Ruth and her parents when her lies are found out.

Scenes 2 and 3 take place in the same setting. How does the author show and tell you that some time has passed between them?

_____

_____

_____

_____

✓ **Here is a sample answer:**

    At the end of scene 2, we see Ruth in the studio in her school clothes, getting an application for a kendo class. In scene 3, we see her in kendo gear and responding to coaching in Japanese, so you know it's happening at a later time. Also, James says that she's been coming to classes for two months.

UNIT 3 ▨▨▨▨▨▨▨▨▨▨▨▨▨▨▨▨▨▨▨▨▨▨▨▨▨▨▨▨▨▨▨▨▨
Craft and Structure

How does the title "Without Flinching" suggest what will happen later in this play?

_____

_____

_____

✓ You get a hint of what the title means in scene 3. James tells Ruth that she must "overcome the natural reaction to flinch," and "cultivate a nonflinching spirit." She hasn't been able to do this, but you know there's something coming at her that will hurt worse than a bamboo stick. Here is a sample answer:

> Ruth knows very well that she has to face the consequences of her lies and that she deserves them. The title suggests that she will face them with "a nonflinching spirit."

Test Yourself

Casey at the Bat

by Ernest Lawrence Thayer

The outlook wasn't brilliant for the Mudville nine that day:
The score stood four to two, with but one inning more to play.
And so when Cooney died at first, and Burrows did the same,
A sickly silence fell upon the patrons of the game.

5   A straggling few got up to go in deep despair. The rest
Clung to that hope which springs eternal in the human breast:
They thought, if only Casey could but get a whack at that—
We'd put up even money, now, with Casey at the bat.

But Flynn preceded Casey, as did also Jimmy Blake,
10 And the former was a lulu and the latter was a cake;
So upon that stricken multitude grim melancholy[1] sat,
For there seemed but little chance of Casey's getting to the bat.

But Flynn let drive a single, to the wonderment of all,
And Blake, the much despised, tore the cover off the ball;
15 And when the dust had lifted, and they saw what had occurred,
There was Jimmy safe at second and Flynn a-hugging third.

Then from 5,000 throats and more there rose a lusty yell;
It rumbled on the mountaintops; it rattled in the dell;
It struck upon the hillside and recoiled upon the flat,
20 For Casey, mighty Casey, was advancing to the bat.

There was ease in Casey's manner as he stepped into his place;
There was pride in Casey's bearing and a smile on Casey's face.
And when, responding to the cheers, he lightly doffed his hat,
No stranger in the crowd could doubt 'twas Casey at the bat.

25 Ten thousand eyes were on him as he rubbed his hands with dirt;
Five thousand tongues applauded when he wiped them on his shirt.
Then while the writhing pitcher ground the ball into his hip,
Defiance gleamed in Casey's eye, a sneer curled Casey's lip.

And now the leather-covered sphere came hurtling through the air,
30 And Casey stood a-watching it in haughty grandeur there.
Close by the sturdy batsman the ball unheeded sped—
"That ain't my style," said Casey. "Strike one," the umpire said.

From the benches, black with people, there went up a muffled roar,
Like the beating of the storm-waves on a stern and distant shore.
35 "Kill him! Kill the umpire!" shouted someone in the stand;
And it's likely they'd a-killed him had not Casey raised his hand.

[1]**melancholy:** feeling of depression

With a smile of Christian charity great Casey's visage[2] shone;
He stilled the rising tumult; he bade the game go on.
He signaled to the pitcher, and once more the spheroid flew;
40 But Casey still ignored it, and the umpire said, "Strike two."

"Fraud!" cried the maddened thousands, and echo answered fraud;
But one scornful look from Casey and the audience was awed.
They saw his face grow stern and cold, they saw his muscles strain,
And they knew that Casey wouldn't let that ball go by again.

45 The sneer is gone from Casey's lip; his teeth are clenched in hate;
He pounds with cruel violence his bat upon the plate.
And now the pitcher holds the ball, and now he lets it go,
And now the air is shattered by the force of Casey's blow.

Oh, somewhere in this favored land the sun is shining bright;
50 The band is playing somewhere, and somewhere hearts are light;
And somewhere men are laughing, and somewhere children shout;
But there is no joy in Mudville—mighty Casey has struck out.

"Casey at the Bat" is a narrative poem. It's a poem that tells a story. Summarize each of these groups of stanzas and explain how it fits with the others to tell the story. Use terms you learned in Lesson 6, such as *conflict* and *rising action*.

1 Stanzas 1–3

_____

_____

_____

2 Stanza 4

_____

_____

_____

3 Stanzas 5–7

_____

_____

_____

[2]**visage:** face

4 Stanzas 8–12

_____

_____

_____

5 Stanza 13

_____

_____

_____

6 Does the way the poem is set up "make you feel like you're at the ball game," or at least like you're watching it on TV? Explain why, or why not.

_____

_____

_____

_____

_____

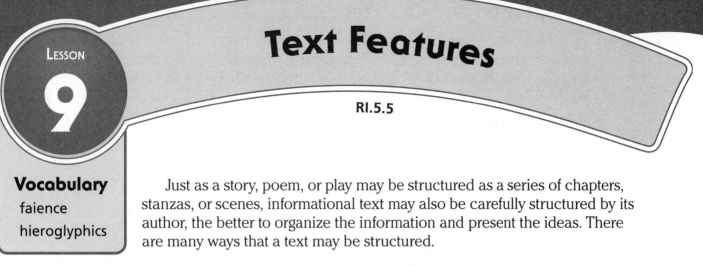

Vocabulary
faience
hieroglyphics

Just as a story, poem, or play may be structured as a series of chapters, stanzas, or scenes, informational text may also be carefully structured by its author, the better to organize the information and present the ideas. There are many ways that a text may be structured.

Sequence and Chronological Order

One way authors organize information is by presenting it as a series of events or steps. When you read, you need to be able to understand the correct **sequence** in which events or steps happen. Whether you are reading about someone's life, programming a cell phone, or baking cookies, you need to follow the sequence.

| You look on the library shelves. | → | You choose a book. | → | You take it to the counter. | → | You check the book out. |

A chronological text is not always written in sequential order. For example, a biography may begin with the subject's death or the moment of her greatest triumph, and then "flashback" to her birth. You can follow the sequence by looking for clues. Watch for words that indicate time, such as *1945, Friday, last May,* and *11:00 p.m.* Look for other words that indicate sequence, too.

Cause and Effect

Another way that authors organize information is by showing connections between ideas and events that explain why things happen. Your reading makes more sense when you understand these *why* connections. Look for clue words that signal **cause and effect.** The thing that happens is the **effect.** The reason why it happens, or what made it happen, is the **cause.** Clue words that signal **causes** include *because, since, reason for, due to,* and *on account of.* Clue words that signal **effects** are *then, so, led to, as a result, in order that,* and *therefore.*

Comparison and Contrast

A third way writers organize information is by pointing out similarities and differences. When you note similarities between two things, actions, or ideas, you're **comparing.** When you note differences between them, you're **contrasting.**

This Venn diagram compares and contrasts two violent storms.

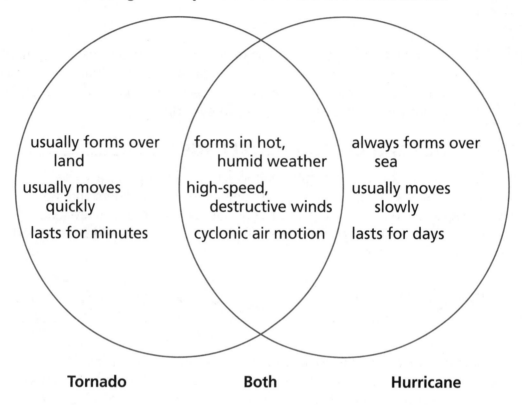

Tornado	Both	Hurricane
usually forms over land	forms in hot, humid weather	always forms over sea
usually moves quickly	high-speed, destructive winds	usually moves slowly
lasts for minutes	cyclonic air motion	lasts for days

The middle of the diagram shows how a tornado and a hurricane are similar. It **compares** the two storms. The outer part of each circle shows how a tornado and a hurricane are different. They **contrast** the two storms.

These are some other ways that authors might choose to organize information:

- as a series of problems and solutions
- as a series of questions and answers
- in order of importance, from greatest to least

Can you think of what kinds of information might be presented best with each of these organizational structures?

Guided Practice

Trouble? Check Your MAXXON SoundStick to Find Out What's Wrong

My SoundStick won't turn on.

- Check whether the battery is charged.

I've recharged the battery, but my SoundStick still won't turn on.

- You may need to reset your SoundStick. Go to www.maxxon. com/support/soundstick and click on the button for your model.

I cannot see the SoundStick icon in iTunes®.

- Try plugging it into a different USB port on your computer.

The SoundStick won't let me download a playlist from iTunes®.

- Make sure you have the latest versions of the SoundStick and iTunes® software installed.

There is no sound, or the sound is distorted.

- Check whether you have your headset or ear pods correctly plugged in.

My SoundStick does not respond to my menu selections.

- Your computer files may have become corrupted or infected by a virus. Scan your hard drive for viruses and spyware.

Some of my SoundStick apps are not working.

- You may need to remove content synched to the application, test, and resynch the content. Connect your SoundStick by USB. Click on the SoundStick icon, then select each tab to change what content is synched. When you are finished, click Apply.

With a group, choose a piece of technology (for example, a video-game machine or cell phone) and research how it works. Prepare a poster or display for your class. How will you organize your information?

How an MP3 Player Works

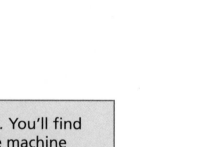

How many music CDs can you fit in your pocket. The answer: about 500—that is, if you have a typical 20GB (gigabyte) MP3 player. This electronic device, smaller than a deck of cards, can store thousands of songs. That's because the MP3 file format compresses electronic information so that it takes much less space.

Compression is the reason much of today's technology works, from digital cameras to DVD players. Like all digital files, a sound file uploaded to a computer from a CD is stored as a long string of ones and zeroes. A four-minute song takes up about 40 MB (megabytes) of space—about 320 million ones and zeroes. An MP3 file squeezes that data into about one-tenth as much space. When you connect a computer to an MP3 player, it transfers the data in that compressed format.

An MP3 player actually is a tiny computer. The music files are stored on a thin hard drive. You hear them as music because a processor inside turns the ones and zeroes back into sound waves. How does it "know" where to find the song or playlist you've selected? That's due to a part called a scroll wheel. It works like a computer's mouse to find the right data.

Convenience is the reason MP3 players are so popular. But something is lost when you carry a music library around in your pocket. That "something" is sound quality. That's due to the nine-tenths of the data that are lost in the compression process. There's a lot of detail in those nine-tenths! Listening to your favorite song on an MP3 player, you probably won't notice. But listening to it again on a CD with a good headset, you'll be sure to hear the difference.

The first passage is organized as a ____.

   A chronological sequence

   B series of causes and effects

   C series of questions and answers

   D series of problems and solutions

> ✓ The first passage is what is known as a *troubleshooting guide.* You'll find one in a manual of instructions for anything from a video-game machine to a gas cooking grill. It helps you deal with problems you can fix yourself. For easy reference, it lists *problems* in the order in which they are likely to come up, together with their solutions. A chronological structure (choice A) wouldn't make sense. A cause-and-effect structure (choice B) would tell you *why* your MP3 player isn't working but not how to fix it. An FAQ structure ("frequently asked questions") would be helpful, but that wasn't the approach the author chose. Choice D is correct.

UNIT 3 ▪▪
Craft and Structure

What do you do if you can't see the SoundStick icon in iTunes®?

_____

_____

> ✓ This question demonstrates why the problem-and-solution organization works well for this kind of text. You simply go down the list of problems until you find the one you're looking for, and note the solution. See how easy it is? Here is a sample answer:

If you can't see the SoundStick icon, then plug the SoundStick into a different USB port on your computer.

The second passage is organized _____.

A in order of importance

B in chronological sequence

C as a series of causes and effects

D as a series of questions and answers

> ✓ The second passage explains how something works. It's not meant to help you fix your MP3 player, but it does take some of the mystery out of its operation. It explains *why* each step happens, from uploading music files to playing them on the MP3 player. Did you catch the cause-and-effect clue words, such as *because* and *due to?* They tell you that you're not reading information in sequence or order of importance, and you can see that there are no questions. Choice C is the correct answer.

Why is the sound quality on a CD better than on an MP3 player?

_____

_____

> The *effect* is that the sound quality of a CD is better. What is the *cause?* Look back at the third paragraph. The clue is the phrase "due to." Read the previous sentences and the following one. You'll see why a cause-and-effect structure is useful for explaining this kind of information. Here is one way to answer the question:

Sound quality is lost in an MP3 file because detail is lost when the data is compressed.

What would be another good way to organize the information in the second passage? Explain why.

_____

_____

_____

_____

> Were you easily able to understand how a MP3 player works by reading the passage? What could have made it plainer? Here is one possible answer:

One way would be to organize the passage as questions and answers. Why does this happen? What causes this to happen? They could help you see the cause-and-effect relationships more clearly, especially if a diagram was included.

Julie Chan, Guitar Maker

When you were a teen, did you dream about building musical instruments?

Julie: No way! I wanted to be the queen of rock and roll, but I didn't want to be just another girl singer. I wanted to play guitar. The trouble was, I was terrible at it. I had no musical sense.

How did you get from playing a guitar to building them?

Julie: What I was good at was working with my hands. My dad had a workshop in the garage. I'd always liked making things with his tools. So when I was 18, I got it into my head to build a guitar.

How do you learn something like that?

Julie: I built my first guitar from instructions in a book. Of course, my first one was…well, shall we say worthy of my playing? But you have to expect that. I took some lessons from a master instrument maker in Tennessee, and I just kept at it till I knew what I was doing….

What's the hardest thing about building a guitar?

Julie: Shaping the sides is tricky. You use a special tool called a bending jig. It's made of aluminum and shaped like the side of a guitar. First, you have to soak the wood in hot water to soften it. I do that for about 10 or 15 minutes, which is about how long it takes for the jig to heat up. Then you clamp the wood tightly to the jig and leave it for another 10 minutes. Then you turn off the jig, wait till it cools, and take the wood off. If you've done it right, it should hold its shape.

What about those crazy-shaped guitars some rockers play? Do you need a special bending jig?

Julie: Oh, for an electric guitar, you can forget all this. The body is made from a single, solid piece of wood.

Which of these *best* describes the overall structure of the information in this article?

A sequence of steps

B causes and effects

C questions and answers

D comparing and contrasting

> This passage has a slightly more complex structure than the ones about MP3 players. One of Julie's responses describes a sequence of steps. But the *overall* structure consists of an interviewer asking questions and Julie answering them. There are no causes and effects and no comparing and contrasting. Choice C is the correct answer.

When she shapes the sides of a guitar, what does Julie do while the bending jig is heating up?

_____

> Julie describes the process of shaping the sides as a sequence of steps. Her describing the process this way helps you picture in your mind how she does it. Here is one way to answer the question:

Julie soaks the wood in hot water to soften it.

How do the three passages in this lesson suggest why writers choose to structure their information in different ways?

_____

_____

_____

_____

_____

_____

_____

✓ Your answer should compare and contrast the organizational structures of the three passages by considering the kind of information that each presents. Here is one possible answer:

You can understand different kinds of information better with different kinds of organization. Julie Chan's information might have been more random and less interesting if an interviewer had just let her talk instead of asking a series of questions. For similar reasons, you would choose a problem-and-solution structure to explain how to fix something, a cause-and-effect approach to explain a process in science, or a chronological structure to describe the events of a person's life.

Test Yourself

Read two passages. Then answer the questions.

Passage 1:

Baseball, Japanese Style

by Elena Castro

It all started with Horace Wilson. He was an American who traveled to Japan in 1872 to teach English in a Japanese school. He also taught his students something else—baseball. The Japanese took to the game at once. By 1878, Wilson's school was being challenged by teams from other schools. Before long, baseball was being played all over Japan.

Japan has a unique culture that is nearly 2,000 years old. After Americans first went there in 1853, the Japanese took a close look at American ways. Some they wanted no part of, but others seem to fit with their way of life. One of these was baseball. Sports had long been part of Japanese culture, but they were individual contests rather than team games. Like the sports of the ancient Greeks, they were forms of mock fighting that developed out of training for battle. In English, we call them martial arts, from a word that means "warlike." The Japanese saw something of the martial arts in baseball. There was the battle between pitcher and batter. There was the need for a strong body and a focused mind. The game involved precise timing and quick action. A team had to play together as if they were one person. A Japanese writer may have said it best: "Baseball is perfect for us. If the Americans hadn't invented it, we probably would have."

The first baseball game between U.S. and Japanese teams was played in 1896. The Japanese won, 29–4. Americans would never again take a Japanese team lightly! Soon American college teams were visiting Japan often, and Japanese teams visited the United States. American major-league teams played in Japan for the first time in 1913. A key event occurred in 1934, when a team of American stars led by Babe Ruth played a series in Japan. Two years later, Japan had its own professional baseball league.

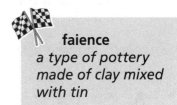

take lightly (idiom) *underestimate, not consider worthy competition*

There are a few differences between Japanese and American baseball. Japanese teams train very hard. (One American player has said, "They think practice is more important than the games!") There can be ties. Teams more often play for one run than for a "big inning." Players bow to each other before the game starts. They almost never question an umpire's call. Japanese players will not "steal signs" from the other team or slide hard into second base to try to break up a double play. In America, these tactics have always been part of the game. In Japan, they are considered dishonorable.

In both countries, it's "one, two, three strikes, you're out." Hitting, fielding, and running are the same. American major-leaguers have been playing on Japanese teams since the 1960s. Japanese stars like Ichiro Suzuki, Hideki Matsui, and Daesuke Matsuzaka have enlivened American baseball since the 1990s.

In 2006, the first-ever World Baseball Classic was held. It matched teams from 16 countries in a tournament like soccer's World Cup. It was won by Japan.

Passage 2:

Tunnel Opened in Pharaoh's Tomb

Another Ancient Treasure Unearthed in Egypt

CAIRO—Egyptian archaeologists announced today that the ancient tunnel they have been excavating since 2007 was meant to connect a 3,300-year-old royal tomb with a secret burial site.

faience *a type of pottery made of clay mixed with tin*

The 570-foot tunnel in the tomb of King Seti I (reigned 1314?–1304? B.C.) was excavated by a team led by Zahi Hawass, Egypt's leading archaeologist. It was cut into the bedrock at the rear of Seti's tomb in Egypt's Valley of the Kings. Dr. Hawass believes that the workers and artists who built the beautifully decorated tomb began afterward to construct the tunnel, but the Pharaoh died before it was completed.

In the tunnel, the archaeologists found ancient figurines, wall carvings, pottery shards, a boat model made of faience, and an inscription apparently written as instructions for the workers by the tomb's architect. Written in hieratic, a simplified form of hieroglyphics, the inscription reads, "Move the door jamb up and make the passage wider." Deeper inside the tunnel, the archaeologists found what appear to be an artist's preliminary sketches for wall decorations.

hieroglyphics *a form of writing that uses pictures to represent ideas and sounds*

The tunnel inside Seti's tomb was originally discovered in 1960. It was excavated at the time to a depth of 443 feet, but the dig was abandoned because the workers found it too hard to breathe. Dr. Hawass's team cleared away the rubble from this earlier dig and were shocked to find a descending passage and two descending staircases. The construction apparently stopped after the second staircase, which was left unfinished. Dr. Hawass concludes that Seti was trying to construct a secret tomb inside his tomb.

Seti I was the second king of Egypt's 19th Dynasty. His military victories restored parts of Egypt's empire that had been lost under previous kings. He fought wars in western Asia, Libya, and Nubia (modern Sudan). His capture of Kadesh (in modern Syria) from the Hittites in the eighth year of his reign is considered his greatest triumph. Archaeologists have long known this history from inscriptions in Seti's tomb, the largest in the Valley of the Kings.

Seti's triumphs were overshadowed by those of his son, the long-reigning Ramesses II. Dr. Hawass believes that Ramesses's tomb may have a secret tunnel like his father's. Locating and excavating it may be Dr. Hawass's next project.

> Ancient Egyptian history recorded no fewer than 30 dynasties (ruling families) of kings and queens, over a period of more than 3,000 years!

1 Which of these *best* describes the overall structure of passage 1?

   A causes and effects

   B questions and answers

   C chronological sequence

   D problems and solutions

2 Which of these *best* describes how the information in passage 2 is organized?

   A in order of importance

   B in chronological order

   C as a series of causes and effects

   D as a series of problems and solutions

UNIT 3
Craft and Structure

3 Explain why the authors of the two passages may have chosen to organize their material the way they did.

_____

_____

_____

_____

_____

4 In "Baseball, Japanese Style," the second paragraph *mainly* ____.

   A   contrasts baseball with Japanese martial arts

   B   compares baseball with ancient Greek sports

   C   compares baseball with Japanese martial arts

   D   contrasts ancient Greek sports with Japanese martial arts

5 Explain how the information in paragraphs 4 and 5 of "Baseball, Japanese Style" is organized.

_____

_____

_____

_____

_____

Point of View and Author's Purpose

RL.5.6, RI.5.6

Vocabulary

dame
portal
scrimmage
squirmed
vanity

Anything ever written has a point of view. In fiction, the story is told from the point of view of a character or of a narrator outside the story. A poem is told from the point of view of the speaker. A play also represents someone's point of view, either a character or the author.

Informational text has a point of view, too. Suppose you're reading about America's War of Independence. A history written in the United States would describe the facts and take the point of view that the outcome was a good thing. A history written in England might describe the same facts but take an entirely different point of view. Suppose you could read George Washington's diary? How about a diary written by a soldier in Washington's army? How about a diary kept by the soldier's wife, back on the farm? Each would express a different point of view. Whatever you're reading, it's important to recognize that the author's point of view and purpose for writing influences the way events are described and topics are explained.

Point of View in Literary Text

Who is telling the story? In some stories, a character is the narrator. This is called the **first-person point of view.** You can recognize a story told in the first person because the narrator uses the pronouns *I* and *we*.

Other stories are told from a **third-person point of view.** The narrator uses pronouns like *he, she,* and *they* to indicate the different characters. A third-person narrator may take the point of view of one or more characters in the story, or of an observer outside the story.

Guided Practice

Read the passage. Then answer the questions.

scrimmage
struggle, or playing a sport for practice

from Teammates

by Harold Marshall

We weren't actually practicing yet, just shooting balls at the netless hoop in our usual goofball coach-isn't-here-yet way, when I saw Rob Smith standing at the edge of the gym watching us. He was wearing shorts and a basketball shirt that he must have borrowed from an adult. It kind of billowed out around him like a sheet on a clothesline on a windy day. Louis and Daniel and Nick, who, like me, knew Rob from school, all kind of gave each other looks like question marks. For the other guys, who went to St. Michael's or Villa, he was just a kid who had wandered into the gym by mistake, like his team had the same practice time except on Tuesday, and he had messed up on what day it was. That would have been just like Rob.

Coach Dave's whistle interrupted our nonpractice. He was standing there next to Rob, so when we came over and sat on the floor around him, we couldn't exactly ignore the presence of the alien among us.

"Hi, Rob."

"Hey."

"What's up, Rob?"

"Hunh."

"Guys, I see that some of you already know Robert Smith," Coach Dave said. "He's joining our team as of today."

There was another round of Hi-Robs from the guys who didn't know him, Coach Dave's kid Jamal included, and a "hey" and a little wave back from Rob. Louis was directly across from me in the half-circle, so I couldn't ignore his look of alarm that was probably a mirror of my own.

"Now, we have our first game Saturday against the Panthers, and we need to work Rob into our system, so let's get started."

So we had the usual drills and shoot-around, and then a four-on-four scrimmage, which would have been four-on-five now with Rob on the team, except Coach Dave joined in on our side. Rob wasn't the worst player on the court, but I knew it wouldn't be long before he started talking like he was the best. When he threw an air ball, I was glad it wasn't baseball we were playing, because he might have picked up a bat and started hitting the backstop and scaring everyone.

Around school there were all kinds of stories about Rob. He lived at the Good Shepherd Children's Home, and we all felt sad for him for not having even one parent or even a grandmother to come home to. He told everyone his parents had been killed in a car crash, and we felt sad about that, too. But Jenny Paul had told me that his parents had actually put him in there because they couldn't handle him, and there were about five different stories about why he wasn't at his old school any more. They couldn't all have been true, but if even one was, it made it kind of hard to feel friendly toward him. I figured Coach Dave must know the stories, too, or else he'd find out soon enough.

What is the point of view of this story?

A first person

B third person, told by a narrator outside the story

C third person, from the point of view of one character

D third person, revealing the thoughts of several characters

> The narrator of the story—we don't know his name—is a character, and he uses the pronouns *I* and *we*. So it's a first-person narrative, not third person. The correct answer is choice A.

How does the narrator's point of view influence how the events in the story are described?

_____

_____

_____

_____

> The key event that happens here is Rob joining the team. The narrator knows Rob from school. Can you separate the facts he tells us from what he *thinks* he knows? Here is a sample answer:

The narrator knows Rob, but he doesn't know him well and is not Rob's friend. He's seen Rob lose his temper in scary ways and has heard scary stories about him. He's worried about what it will be like to have Rob on his team.

UNIT 3
Craft and Structure

Read this sentence about the passage.

I know Rob is a troubled child, and I have to make him feel like he's part of the team.

Whose point of view does this sentence express?

    A   the coach

    B   the narrator

    C   one of the other boys who knows Rob

    D   one of the boys who doesn't know Rob

> If a story is told from one character's point of view, you may have to infer what other characters are thinking. You already know what the narrator thinks. Does the statement sound like anything one of the boys would think, whether or not they know Rob? Consider what a tough job Coach Dave will have if the stories about Rob are true. The answer is choice A.

Write a sentence that Rob might be thinking in the story.

_____

_____

> Your answer depends on how you feel about Rob. Is he the scary kid the narrator describes, a sad and lonely boy, or a different kind of person entirely? Here is a sample answer that might express Rob's point of view:

I know some of these guys don't like me, so they're going to make the other guys not like me.

The Glove and the Lions

by Leigh Hunt

King Francis was a hearty king, and loved a royal sport;
And one day, as his lions fought, sat looking on the court:
The nobles filled the benches round, the ladies by their side,
And 'mongst them sat the Count de Lorge, with one for whom
    he sighed;
5 And truly 'twas a gallant thing to see that crowning show—
Valor and love, and a king above, and the royal beasts below.

Ramp'd and roar'd the lions, with horrid laughing jaws;
They bit, they glared, gave blows like beams—a wind went with their paws:
With wallowing might and stifled roar, they rolled on one another,
10 Till all the pit, with sand and mane, was in a thunderous smother;
The bloody foam above the bars came whizzing through the air;
Said Francis then, "Faith! Gentlemen, we're better here than there!"

De Lorge's love o'erheard the King—a beauteous lively dame,[1]
With smiling lips and sharp bright eyes, which always seem'd the same:
15 She thought, "The Count my lover is brave as brave can be—
He surely would do wondrous things to show his love of me:
Kings, ladies, lovers, all looked on; the occasion is divine"
I'll drop my glove, to prove his love: great glory will be mine!"

She dropped her glove to prove his love, then looked at him and smiled;
20 He bowed, and in a moment leapt among the lions wild.
The leap was quick, return was quick, he has regain'd his place,
Then threw the glove—but not with love—right in the lady's face!
"In truth," cried Francis, "rightly done!" and rose from where he sat.
"No love," quoth he, "but vanity,[2] sets love a task like that!"

This poem is set in the 1500s. Find out about Leigh Hunt and when he lived. What point of view might a writer today express about the events Hunt describes?

---

[1]**dame:** lady, woman of noble birth

[2]**vanity:** too much pride in one's own self

UNIT 3
Craft and Structure

134

What is the point of view of this poem?

A first person

B third person, told by a narrator outside the story

C third person, from the point of view of one character

D third person, revealing the thoughts of several characters

> There is no *I* in this poem, which rules out choice A. The speaker tells you what the lady is thinking, but he certainly is not expressing her point of view (choice C) or those of the other characters (choice D). The speaker observes and reports what he sees and hears. The correct answer is choice B.

Write a sentence that expresses the point of view of the lady.

_____

_____

> What would the lady tell us if she were the speaker in the poem? You don't know. You have to trust what the speaker tells you, or else you're imposing your own point of view. The speaker tells you that the lady's eyes don't reveal her feelings (line 14). He tells you what she thinks and does (lines 15–19). And he tells you how de Lorge and King Francis respond. Here is a sample answer:

If Count de Lorge really loves me, he'll jump into the pit with the lions to pick up my glove.

Describe the events of the poem from your own point of view.

_____

_____

_____

_____

_____

_____

_____

> You've read the poem, and your point of view is as valid as anyone else's is—whether a character in the poem, the speaker, or the poet. Here is one possible answer:

A king and his lords and ladies are watching two lions fight. One lady wants to test how much Count de Lorge loves her, so she drops her glove in the pit with the lions. He jumps in and picks up the glove, but then he throws it in the lady's face. The king approves, saying that what the lady did proves she doesn't really love the count at all. I think they all should have something thrown in their faces for enjoying such an awful "sport."

Point of View in Informational Text

In informational text, the point of view is the author's. But the author may have different reasons for writing. An author's purpose will be reflected in his point of view. Two people writing about the same event or topic may have entirely different purposes and different points of view.

Think of an article about a movie you've been waiting to see. It may talk about the actors and some of the exciting scenes. The author of this article is probably writing to **inform** or **explain.**

Now think of a review of the same movie, written by a critic. It's her job to discuss the movie's bad points as well as its good points, and to recommend whether or not people should see it. What about an ad for the movie, written by someone at the company that made it? The reviewer and the advertiser are both writing to **persuade.**

Now imagine that you've just seen the movie. You write an e-mail to your friend telling him about the special effects. Chances are you're writing to **describe.**

UNIT 3 ▨▨▨▨▨▨▨▨▨▨▨▨▨▨▨▨▨▨▨▨▨▨▨▨▨▨▨▨▨▨▨▨▨▨▨▨▨▨
136
Craft and Structure

Guided Practice

Read two passages. Then answer the questions.

Whose Game Is It Anyway?

by Richard Gibbs

Board games go back more than 3,000 years. Find out about and play a board game that was popular in ancient Egypt, or one that was popular in the Middle Ages.

Charles Darrow's story is an American legend. Darrow was a heater salesman from Pennsylvania. During the Great Depression of the 1930s, he, like millions of others, lost his job. While taking odd jobs to feed his family, Darrow invented a board game. It was a property-trading game. Players bought and sold properties represented by spaces on the board. Darrow named them after streets in the beach resort town of Atlantic City, New Jersey, where his family had vacationed in better days. Darrow's family and friends played the game at his kitchen table. His friends liked it so much that they asked him to make sets for them. He and his family made the boards by hand on pieces of oilcloth. As more people bought them, he had them printed on cardboard. He sold sets to a Philadelphia department store. When he first tried to sell his idea to game companies, they weren't interested. But when more stores bought his sets, they took notice. In 1935, Parker Brothers paid Darrow for the rights to publish his game. "Monopoly" became the most popular board game in America, and Darrow became the first millionaire game designer.

As with most legends, however, the real story is not so simple. Darrow indeed put the finishing touches on the game we know as Monopoly, but he based it on earlier board games. Elizabeth Magie had invented "The Landlord's Game" in 1904. Its board and basic idea were very like Monopoly's. Another similar game was called "The Fascinating Game of Finance," later shortened to "Finance." It was developed in the 1920s by an Indianapolis woman named Ruth Hoskins and her friends. In 1929, Hoskins moved to Atlantic City to teach school. She developed a version of her game using that city's street names. The board included four railroads and a jail. Players collected $200 as they passed a space called "Go." A man named Charles Todd learned the game in Atlantic City. He taught it to his friend—Charles Darrow.

But legends have a way of replacing fact. Charles Darrow is usually given sole credit for inventing Monopoly. Today, the game is published in many languages and in hundreds of versions. The boards represent foreign cities, sports teams, even imaginary lands. More money is printed for the game each year than all the real money printed by all the countries in the world. In Atlantic City, there stands a monument to Charles Darrow, "inventor" of Monopoly. It stands on the Boardwalk, at the corner of Park Place.

How to Win at Monopoly

by Lydia Bedell

Want to be a killer Monopoly player? Then forget everything you think you know about the game. If you think it's just a matter of the luck of the dice and picking the most expensive properties, you're going to lose. I always did when I was a kid, until I read about two guys who had programmed a computer to analyze the game. After that, I won so regularly that none of my friends wanted to play with me any more.

Some of the conclusions of these computer whizzes should be fascinating to any Monopoly player. You think Boardwalk and Park Place are the best monopoly to own? Think again! There are only two of them, while most sets have three properties. That means after you've spent your money on hotels, the chance that someone will land on them is only two-thirds as great as his landing on the green properties up the street. What about the cards that say, "Advance to Go"? Players who draw them will miss your high-priced real estate entirely. They'll come all the way around the board before you have a chance to collect. Watch out for the cop in the corner—that corner that says, "Go to jail." Players that land there aren't going to be visiting your high-rent district for a while either.

In fact, for that very reason, the best properties to own are those on the half of the board between "Jail" and "Go to jail." What's the very best monopoly? That would be the red set just clockwise of "Free Parking." What makes that the best set to own? In the long run, over many rolls of the dice, those properties will bring you the best return on your money. That's the way real-estate owners figure profits in the real world—how much they're likely to get back over what they spend.

A few other tips I learned from that article: The railroads are good to own early on, but once most of the properties have been bought up, trade your odd railroad for a deed that will give you one of the better colored monopolies. Trade two. It's worth it, even if it gives your sister all four railroads. Don't be picky early in the game. Buy up everything you land on, even the utilities. Otherwise, someone else will get them.

Oh yes, and Free Parking? By the game's official rules, that's just a neutral space, but everyone in the known universe uses the unwritten rule that you get cash from the bank when you land on it. That causes what economists call *inflation*. Playing by the strict rules won't help anybody win, but it will keep the game from going on for six hours.

Which of these *best* expresses Richard Gibbs's point of view?

A Board games are a foolish waste of time.

B It's interesting to know the history of games.

C Charles Darrow stole the idea for Monopoly.

D Monopoly is so famous that there's a monument to its inventor.

> Do you ever wonder who invented any of your favorite games? Richard Gibbs has. He seems to like Monopoly as well as anybody (choice A). He's not saying that Mr. Darrow should "Go directly to jail" (choice C) or commenting on whether Darrow is worthy of a monument (choice D). He thinks the story behind the game is interesting, though, and he thinks you should, too. The correct answer is choice B.

Write a sentence that expresses Lydia Bedell's point of view.

_____

> Lydia Bedell seems to be a woman who enjoys games. She likes to win, but winning isn't as important to her as understanding the inner workings of the game that give her a better chance. Her point of view is that these tricks of strategy "should be fascinating to any Monopoly player." Here is one possible answer:

Monopoly is more fun if you know some strategy.

Compare and contrast the points of view and purposes for writing that the two passages represent.

_____

_____

_____

_____

_____

_____

_____

✓ The two authors are writing on the same topic, yet their interests in Monopoly appear to be completely different. Here is one way to answer the question:

Mr. Gibbs's details are concerned with the business of the game—who invented it, who *really* invented it, its popularity, and the amount of Monopoly money printed each year. Ms. Bedell couldn't care less about that; her details are about how the game is played. She likes the idea that someone programmed a computer to analyze it. But both authors have the same purpose for writing: to explain something interesting about the game. They both take the point of view that the game is fun and that people enjoy playing it.

UNIT 3 ▒▒▒▒▒▒▒▒▒▒▒▒▒▒▒▒▒▒▒▒▒▒▒▒▒▒▒▒▒▒▒▒▒▒▒▒
Craft and Structure

Test Yourself

Read two passages. Then answer the questions.

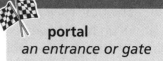

portal
an entrance or gate

from **Choices**

by Leslie Miller

I spent that summer working in a factory that made parts for air conditioners. It was never less than 90 degrees inside. The roar of the machinery was like the sound inside the subway tunnel when a train was passing through. It never let up, except for the half hour they gave us for lunch.

It was the summer before my senior year. There were about a dozen of us high-school kids working there. At lunch we kept mostly to ourselves. Mostly we griped about the working conditions and the supervisors, but there was a lot of mindless putting down of the factory lifers, too. They were mostly people from Asia or Central America. We could hear them jabbering away at other tables in Spanish or Laotian. The Americans came mostly from small towns in Kentucky and West Virginia. They seemed just as foreign as the foreigners, with their accents and their country music. Willow, whose machine was next to mine, was one of these. She sang constantly as she stuffed the coils of flexible tubing into frames, sad love songs and church hymns. She had a fine voice, from what I could hear above the din of the machinery. She wasn't much older than I was, but she had three kids, whose pictures were taped above her machine. She was pleased when I asked her about them and when I complimented her singing, but otherwise we hardly spoke.

Just beyond the loading dock was a door that led into the area where the offices were. It was after I'd been working there about a month that I had occasion to pass through this heavenly portal, to deliver something to one of the managers. It was so cool and quiet on the other side! I could almost imagine I could hear a brook gurgling and birds twittering. The floor was carpeted, not concrete. My own voice, pitched at factory level, sounded embarrassingly loud.

There are moments when I am not so stupid. All my life I'd been hearing my teachers' work-hard, get-good-grades rap as so much background noise. Yeah, sure. Gimme that remote. Where's the party? Standing with my hand on the doorknob, ready to chain myself to my workstation for the rest of the day, I now saw clearly that I had a choice. I'd always had a choice. The subway tunnel or the cool, quiet glade. On one side of the door, the place where air-conditioner parts were made. On the other side, the place where money was made.

I thought about that all afternoon. I looked at Willow singing to her children's pictures and wondered whether she knew she had a choice, or if she'd even had one to begin with. I wondered how long I would still have one before I found that door slammed in my face forever.

from **Lost at Home**

by Ann Piers

She didn't see her grandpa very often, since it took about an hour to get to him by train. Sylvie and her mother lived in the suburbs, while he had an apartment in the city. He didn't drive any more either, not since he'd lost his sight in one eye, so Sylvie had come to know the scenery between Maysville and the city pretty well. At one end, it was modern office buildings and shopping malls and houses like theirs. At the other, near the station, it was old wooden houses and brick factories, freight yards and smokestacks. In the middle, though, the train passed by a marsh full of birds, and here and there were old farmhouses on hills. Sylvie would always look for those houses. Her grandpa had told her that when he was a boy, the suburb where she lived with her mother was all corn and dairy cows. Sometimes Sylvie wished it still was.

Grandpa met her at the station with a smile and a hug. He took her bag, and together they walked through the downtown streets. As usual, he didn't say much. He let Sylvie chatter on about school, a painting she was doing, and her cousins' visit. Only when they got to the restaurant did she shut up long enough to catch her breath. Grandpa smiled, raised his water glass in a toast, and said,

"Well, here's to the world traveler," he said.

Sylvie would rather have brought it up at his apartment, after lunch, but there it was. "Grandpa, I—I don't want to go to Singapore," she blurted.

"Don't want to go!" he said. "Why on earth not?"

"'Cause it's hot there. All my friends are in Maysville. And I don't speak Singaporese, or whatever they speak there."

"But it's only for two years. What an adventure it will be!"

"Why can't I live with you?"

Grandpa squirmed in his chair. He adjusted his collar. "Sylvie, honey, you know your mom has an important job. Her company has decided she has to go overseas. It'll be fun."

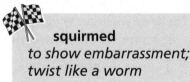

squirmed
to show embarrassment; twist like a worm

"Grandpa, I saw the passport applications this morning. I wanted to hide them, or at least change my address to yours. Even if I lived here with you, I wouldn't be too far from my friends."

Grandpa sighed and ate a French fry. "Sylvie, you don't want to live downtown," he said. "There are no schools. There's nowhere to play. My apartment—it's just too small. Besides, what would you eat? I'm no cook." He lifted his briefcase onto the table. "Here, I've got a little going-away present for you."

That was when Sylvie jumped up from the table and ran, sobbing, for the restroom.

1 What is the point of view of "Choices"?

   A first person

   B third person, told by a narrator outside the story

   C third person, from the point of view of one character

   D third person, revealing the thoughts of several characters

2 What is the point of view of "Lost at Home"?

   A first person

   B third person, told by a narrator outside the story

   C third person, from the point of view of one character

   D third person, revealing the thoughts of several characters

3 In "Choices," how does the narrator's point of view influence how she talks about the factory and her job? How might Willow see things differently?

_____

_____

_____

_____

_____

4 In "Lost at Home," how does Sylvie's point of view influence the events of the story? How might the scene in the restaurant be different if her grandfather were the narrator?

_____

_____

_____

_____

_____

5 Suppose the narrator from "Choices" could meet Sylvie from "Lost at Home." How might she see Sylvie's situation?

_____

_____

_____

_____

_____

REVIEW

Craft and Structure

Vocabulary

amphitheater
oath
oppression
portable
prolific
steward

Read the passage. Then answer the questions.

Many copies of this tale have been found in Egypt, dating back more than 4,000 years.

The Peasant and the Workman

a tale from ancient Egypt

Chapter 1

Power is a poison of the heart. Give a man the slightest dose of it, and see how it turns him rotten! So it has been since the earth first separated from the sky. But every now and then the arm of justice may reach out to overturn the proud and raise up the humble.

In the days when Neb-ka-n-ra was king, no one could have been more humble than a poor peasant who lived with his family in the Salt Country. He traded in salt, rushes, and the other products of his country and brought them to market in the capital.

Now, it happened that his way to market took him past the lands of Meruitensa, high steward of the king. Standing on the bank of a canal was the workman Tehuti-Nekht, son of Asri, a servant of the high steward's. He coveted the peasant's meager goods and his donkeys, and he plotted a way to steal them. He laid a shawl across the narrow path that the trader must travel so that the fastening was in the canal and the fringe in his wheat field on the other side.

As the salt trader approached Tehuti-Nekht said, "Watch out, peasant, that you don't trample on my clothes!"

The trader said, "I will do as you ask; I will go around." He led his donkeys onto the edge of the fields.

The workman said, "Going through my field now, instead of following the path?" The peasant replied, "It is not my choice but the one you left me."

steward
someone who manages another's property or business dealings

Then one of the peasant's donkeys helped itself to a mouthful of the grain. "Look you, peasant, your donkey is eating my wheat, and you will pay full measure! That donkey now is mine!"

The peasant replied, "I am going carefully; the way is blocked; therefore I took my donkeys into the field, and you would seize them for a cluster of wheat? Besides, I know that this land belongs to the high steward Meruitensa! It is he who punishes robbers so harshly; shall I then be robbed on his own land?"

Tehuti-Nekht said, "As the saying goes, 'A poor man owns nothing but his name.' *I* am the high steward of whom you speak!" He took branches of a tamarisk tree and beat the poor peasant about his limbs and back, and he took the peasant's donkeys and turned them into his own pasture. The poor man wept in his pain and cried out.

"Hold your tongue, peasant, or you shall go to the demon of silence!" the workman said.

But the peasant replied, "You beat me and rob me, and now you would take away my voice? Demon of Silence, I will hold my tongue when you restore my goods!"

1 Which of these *best* describes the conflict in this story?

A The peasant is trying to avoid paying his taxes.

B The peasant is trying to get his goods to market.

C The workman is trying to protect the king's lands.

D The peasant seeks justice for the workman's abuse and robbery.

2 What is the point of view of this story?

    A first person

    B third person, told by a narrator outside the story

    C third person, from the point of view of one character

    D third person, revealing the thoughts of several characters

3 How does this chapter build suspense and tension?

_____

_____

_____

_____

_____

4 How would the peasant describe the events of this chapter?

_____

_____

_____

_____

_____

5 What will *most likely* happen in the next chapter?

    A The peasant will go home poorer than ever.

    B The peasant will complain to the high steward.

    C The peasant will use a trick to get back his goods.

    D The peasant will kill the workman and take back his goods.

Chapter 2

The peasant continued on his way to the capital to complain. He found the high steward Meruitensa himself leaving his house to get into his boat that would take him to the judgment hall.

The peasant said, "Stop, please, that I might speak to you of justice! I would ask you to appoint one of your officials that I might send him to you to plead my case for me."

So the high steward ordered one of his officials to hear the peasant's complaint. This man reported back to him later that day as the steward sat among his nobles.

"Behold," said a noble, "let this peasant bring witnesses as is our custom. If this workman Tehuti-Nekht really has done as he says, he should be punished." But Meruitensa held his peace and would not reply to the nobles; he would reply only to the peasant.

So the peasant came to appeal before the high steward, and he said:

> "O my lord steward, greatest of the great,
> When you sail on the lake of truth,
> May you sail upon it with a fair wind,
> May your sail not fly loose,
> May there be no weeping in the cabin,
> May bad luck not follow you,
> May the wave not seize you,
> May you not taste the dirt of the river,
> May you not see the face of fear,
> For you are father to the orphan,
>   husband to the widow.
> Let me celebrate your name in this land:
> A leader without greed in his heart,
> A great one with no meanness,
> Destroyer of lies, champion of justice,
> Hearing the cry, allowing the poor to speak.
> Let me speak; may you listen and give justice:
> Drive oppression from the land, for I am
>   oppressed;
> Judge me; behold, I am cheated."

oppression
the unjust act of being kept down by a higher authority

The high steward Meruitensa went away straight to Neb-ka-n-ra the king. He said, "My lord, a peasant has come before me, most excellent of speech, to complain that his goods were stolen."

The king said, "Continue to listen to his speeches, but do not reply. Bring me his words in writing that I may listen to them. Meanwhile, give him a daily allowance of food and drink, and send likewise to his family."

The high steward did as the king commanded, through a friend so that the peasant would not know from whom his bounty came.

6 Which structural element of the story does this chapter include?

   A climax

   B resolution

   C rising action

   D inciting incident

7 This chapter *best* reveals the high steward to be ____.

   A a just and thoughtful man

   B anxious not to offend his king

   C willing to let others do his work for him

   D angered by the way his workman has treated the peasant

8 Summarize the events of this chapter from the high steward's point of view.

_____

_____

_____

_____

_____

9 Will the peasant get justice? Explain why, or why not. Use details from *both* chapters to support your answer.

_____

_____

_____

_____

_____

Chapter 3

The peasant came again to the high steward, and even a third time, but Meruitensa told two of his followers to seize him and beat him with sticks. The peasant came back again and again, even a sixth time, and he said,

> "My Lord Steward,
>
> Destroying lies and encouraging justice,
>
> Raising up all good things and crushing every evil;
>
> As plenty comes, chasing away famine,
>
> As clothing covers nakedness,
>
> As a clear sky after a storm warms the shivering,
>
> As water quenches thirst,
>
> Turn your face upon my cause; do what is right
>   and not wicked."

But still Meruitensa appeared not to listen to his complaint, even to the ninth time.

At last, however, the high steward sent two of his followers to the peasant and brought him before him. The peasant trembled, thinking he was to be beaten again. But the high steward said to him, "Fear not, peasant, for what you have done. You have made many speeches, delightful to the heart of the king, and I take an oath—as I eat bread and as I drink water—that you will be remembered forever."

oath
a promise

Then Meruitensa raised up the peasant. He took away all the property and privileges of the workman Tehuti-Nekht and gave them to the peasant, who from that time lived with all his family at the king's palace. And the peasant became the chief overseer of Neb-ka-n-ra and stood greatly in his favor for the rest of his days.

10 Write a summary of the events of this chapter of the story.

_____

_____

_____

_____

_____

UNIT 3 ▨▨▨▨▨▨▨▨▨▨▨▨▨▨▨▨▨▨▨▨▨▨▨▨▨▨▨▨▨▨▨▨
Craft and Structure

Passage 1

Backpacking in Olympic National Park

by Emily Browning

My family had done three-day weekend backpacking trips before, but nothing so ambitious as our trek in Olympic National Park. We went at the beginning of summer vacation, when days are longest. Our first adventure was simply getting there. It took all day. Since the starting and ending points of our hike would be 26 miles apart, we had to take both my parents' cars. There was a two-hour wait at the ferry dock. The shortest distance to the Olympic Mountains from Seattle is across the water, and on summer weekends the boats are always crowded. Then we drove several hours to Sol Duc Hot Springs, where our hike would end. We left Dad's car in the parking lot at the trailhead, loaded all our gear into Mom's car, and drove another two hours to the Hoh Rain Forest campground. It was a treat seeing elk grazing by the river as we drove in. We had a feast that night, cooked over a campfire. The only food we would have for the next five days was what we could carry in our packs and cook on a portable stove.

Early the next morning, after getting our backcountry permits from the ranger station, we set off hiking up the Hoh River. This was the longest day's hike, nearly nine miles, but it was also the easiest. It was a gentle slope uphill through the beautiful rain forest. There were more shades of green than I could imagine. The trees were all hung with moss. Red, orange, and purple fungi seemed to sprout out of the rocks. We camped far up the valley in the shadow of the mountains, where we would be for the next three nights.

The second day out, Monday, was the hardest. We hiked less than six miles, but it was almost straight up—about 4,000 feet up. Imagine climbing a steep and endless staircase made of rocks. We stopped to rest often, but still my legs were rubber by the time I dragged them into camp beside Hoh Lake. But I couldn't rest yet. I had to filter water with our little hand pump, as the lake water wasn't safe to drink. (That was my job every place we stopped. By the end of the trip I had developed

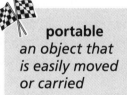

portable
an object that is easily moved or carried

some real muscle from all that pumping!) Then Dad set up the tent, and by the time we had caught our breath, Mom had whipped up a delicious camp supper. After cleanup, we put all our food in one bag and hung it over the limb of a tree so bears couldn't get at it. We didn't see any bears the whole trip, but you don't take chances! We fell asleep at twilight to the music of the lake lapping against the shore.

The next day we were all sore, but there was still more climbing to do. Fortunately, it was only a thousand feet or so. Then we came down into Seven Lakes Basin, and after a short hike arrived at our campsite at Lunch Lake—right about lunchtime. It was warm, but there were still patches of deep snow here and there. We had a snowball fight, which was funny, because it was June. We spent the rest of that day and all the next just hanging out, washing and drying our clothes, watching the deer that came down to the lake to drink and taking short walks. There's a ranger station there, and I had a nice talk with the ranger. Her name was Rachel, and she was spending the whole summer in the park. She shared with us some trout she had caught. Dad fried them on our little camp stove, and no fish ever tasted so delicious.

On the last day, Thursday, we had another eight miles to hike. Once we climbed out of the basin, though, it was all downhill. We passed the time playing word games, and around three in the afternoon we reached the end of the trail and Dad's car. We had two nights' reservations at Sol Duc Hot Springs. Before I could soak in the pools, I had to shower off five days worth of dirt. I could have stayed in that shower all day, it felt so good! The only walking I did for the next two days was between our cabin, the pools, and the restaurant. By Saturday, we were all more than ready to be home.

Passage 2

Wonders of the Hoh

by Don Gianelli

The Hoh Rain Forest in Olympic National Park is one of nature's wonders. The prolific rainfall of the Northwest Coast is especially heavy in the Hoh and other nearby valleys because the Olympic Mountains serve as a barrier to storm clouds moving in off the ocean. Rainfall here averages nearly 200 inches per year. As a result, the Hoh boasts an almost unique environment—the temperate rain forest. Unlike most of Earth's rain forests, which are found in tropical lands near the equator, the Hoh rarely gets hot enough to feel uncomfortable.

Due to the prolific rainfall, the Hoh is crowded with a stunning variety of plant life. The ground is carpeted with ferns and flowers the entire year, the branches of the trees weighted with moss. Because of the almost constant drip, forest fires rarely occur. So the cedar, alder, hemlock, Sitka spruce, and Douglas fir trees here are the tallest of their species on Earth. The rapid decay of plant material in the moist environment yields an almost unearthly assortment of fungi. Brightly colored mushrooms the size of pizzas spring from the forest floor and even from tree trunks. Does green have a smell to it? If it does, it probably smells like the Hoh Rain Forest.

prolific
an abundance of something

Passage 3

Dear Editors:

My family has vacationed in Olympic National Park every summer for 12 years, but this year will be the last unless the state and federal governments act. Getting to the park has become such a headache that it hardly seems worth it. On summer weekends, the wait for the ferry can be endless. We got to the terminal at 9 a.m. and still had to wait in a hot car for four hours before we could get on a boat. There's an easy and obvious fix for this: Put more ferries in service on the route on Saturdays and Sundays during summer. That's what the bus companies do at peak times. It shouldn't cost the taxpayers any extra money, since the crossing fare will cover the costs.

Once we got to the park, we found that services had been cut to the bone. The visitor's center at Hurricane Ridge was closed both times we stopped there. The evening nature talks by the rangers in the amphitheater, which my kids love, were held only on weekends. The rangers mostly seem to be posted in the backcountry. That's fine for backpackers, but what about us campground users? The government ought to restore the funds they've cut from the National Park Service. Maybe they could hire college students for summer work, like keeping the campgrounds clean, so that more rangers would be available for the nature program as well as emergency services. And maybe the Park Service could raise entrance fees. Fifteen bucks instead of ten would still be a bargain for a week in this jewel of nature.

Douglas Gale
Redmond

amphitheater
a round gathering space with seats rising from the center to create different levels

11 How is the information in passage 1 organized?

   A in chronological order

   B as a series of causes and effects

   C as a series of questions and answers

   D as a series of problems and solutions

12 The information in passage 2 is *mainly* presented ____.

   A in chronological order

   B as a series of causes and effects

   C in order of importance, from greatest to least

   D as a comparison and contrast of two environments

13 The author of passage 3 organizes his information ____.

   A in no particular order

   B as a series of causes and effects

   C as a series of problems and solutions

   D in order of importance, from greatest to least

14 The authors of all three passages would agree that Olympic National Park ____.

   A is a great place to visit

   B needs better protection

   C is mostly for backpackers

   D is like an open-air science lab

15 Compare and contrast the purposes of the authors for writing the three passages. How does each author's purpose reflect his or her organizational structure and point of view?

_____

_____

_____

_____

_____

UNIT 3 ▓▓▓
Craft and Structure

Integration of Knowledge and Ideas

As you read, you absorb information from many sources. Reading two or more texts on the same topic can give you more information and different ways of looking at the topic than reading only one. It can also give you insights about the accuracy of the information you're reading, as you evaluate the evidence it presents in support of its points. Visual aids, too, such as maps and illustrations, can add meaning and depth to a text. Noting similarities and differences among stories of the same and different kinds can add to your enjoyment and understanding of literary texts.

This unit is all about how you, the reader, absorbs information and ideas from what you read and combine it with information and ideas from other sources to come up with new insights.

- **In Lesson 11,** you'll learn how visual aids can add to the meaning, tone, or beauty of a literary text, how visual elements can add meaning and depth to the ideas in informational texts, and how reading two or more texts on the same topic can help you more easily to answer questions and solve problems related to the topic.

- **Lesson 12** is about evidence in informational text. You'll learn how to distinguish between facts and an author's opinions, and how to evaluate whether or not the facts are supported by evidence and the opinions by solid reasons—in other words, whether you can trust that the information you're reading is accurate and true.

- **Lesson 13** is about kinds, or *genres,* of literature. You already know the differences among poems, plays, and stories. In this lesson, you'll learn about different types of stories and how to recognize appreciate the similarities and differences within and among them.

Visual Literacy

RL.5.7, RI.5.7, RI.5.9

Vocabulary
famine
sparse
spires

You've probably heard the expression, "A picture is worth a thousand words." An illustration, photograph, graph, or map can add information and meaning to a text that would not be as easy to understand through text alone. When you read two or more sources about the same topic, each with its own visual material, you have more tools available to answer a question or solve a problem.

Guided Practice

Read the passage. Then answer the questions.

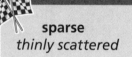

sparse
thinly scattered

Desert Swarm

by Abbas Samhadi

One of the most feared insects on Earth is the desert locust. It lives in the grasslands of northern Africa and southwest Asia. Most of the time, desert locusts don't bother anyone. They feed on the sparse grass of their homeland. When rain falls, however, the grass grows more abundantly. When that happens, the desert locust practically transforms itself into a different insect. The females lay more eggs in the sandy soil. When they hatch, the young locusts gather in large groups to feed. When their hind legs bump against each other, changes take place in their body chemistry. They change in color from green and brown to black, yellow, and pink. They give off a scent that causes them to swarm and fly off in search of food.

A locust swarm can be as small as a square mile or as large as several hundred square miles. A swarm that large darkens the sky. In each square mile, there may be anywhere from 60 million to 80 million locusts. One swarm is said to have had 250 *billion* locusts.

Locusts fly with the wind, so a swarm can travel as fast as the wind is moving. They can stay in the air for long periods of time. They can't fly much higher than 6,000 feet above sea level, so mountains can sometimes block their flight. But some swarms travel hundreds of miles. They can reach as far as Russia, Spain, and India. During the 1987–1989 outbreak, a swarm of locusts from Africa even crossed the Atlantic Ocean to the Caribbean region.

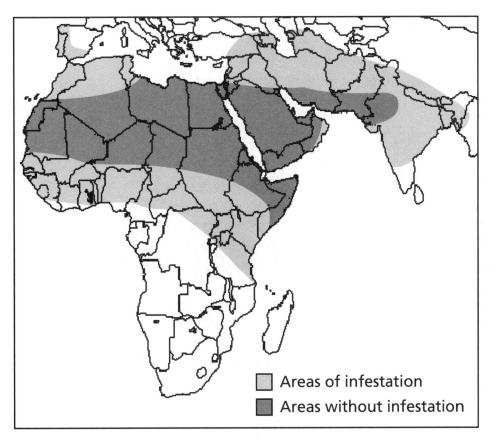

Areas of infestation

Areas without infestation

Regions affected by the 2003–2005 desert locust swarms

Locusts do not bite people or animals, but they eat just about any kind of plant. A single desert locust can eat its weight every day. Even a small swarm can eat three tons of food in a single day. They can breed up to five times a year. Each generation may have ten to 16 times as many locusts as the last. One out of every ten people on Earth lives in danger of famine because of desert locusts. An outbreak in West Africa in 2004 led to severe food shortages in the region.

Locust species are found over most of the world. The Rocky Mountain locust was once as destructive as the desert locust. In the 1870s, it caused enormous crop damage in the central United States. However, by 1902 it had mysteriously gone extinct.

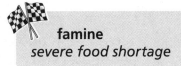

famine
severe food shortage

Desert Locust Plagues, 1910–2010		
Years of Outbreaks		
1926–1934	1949–1963	1987–1989
1940–1948	1967–1969	2003–2005

Which of these facts is *best* illustrated by the photograph on page 156?

A When they hatch, the young locusts gather in large groups to feed.

B Each generation may have ten to 16 times as many locusts as the last.

C They can stay in the air for long periods of time and travel hundreds of miles.

D One out of every ten people on Earth lives in danger of famine because of desert locusts.

> Did the photograph help you understand any facts in the article better than the text alone? It shows locusts feeding on a plant—lots of locusts. The photo doesn't show how fast they breed, how far they fly, or how they endanger humans. But it does give you an idea of what a *swarm* means, and how they eat. Now multiply that photo by several million. Choice A is the correct answer.

The map can help you understand ____.

A how fast a locust swarm can travel

B which countries suffered the worst famine

C how many locusts covered the region in 2003–2005

D which countries were affected by the 2003–2005 outbreak

> Just as the photo gives you an idea of what a locust swarm looks like, the map shows you how large an area was affected by the most recent outbreak. It does not give data on the famine, the size of the swarm, or how fast they traveled. However, by comparing the map with one that shows the names of countries, you can tell which ones were troubled by the outbreak. Choice D is the correct answer.

How does the chart "Desert Locust Plagues, 1910–2010" add meaning to the information in the article?

_____

_____

_____

✓ **The photo, map, and chart each give different kinds of information. Here is one possible answer:**

The article describes what happens during an outbreak of locusts, while the chart shows you how often outbreaks happen and how long they last.

Using information from the article, how could you explain why some areas on the map experienced locust outbreaks while others did not?

_____

_____

✓ **The article gives facts about locusts that can help you explain the map. Here is a sample answer:**

The locusts probably left the area in the middle of the map alone because they couldn't find food there.

Grasshoppers Gone Wild

by Peter Minner

In her novel *On the Banks of Plum Creek,* Laura Ingalls Wilder described the devastation of her Minnesota prairie home by Rocky Mountain locusts. As she wrote:

> *"A cloud was over the sun. It was not like any cloud they had seen before. It was a cloud of something like snowflakes, and thin and glittering. Light shown through each flickering particle....*
>
> *The Cloud was hailing grasshoppers. The cloud was grasshoppers. Their bodies hid the sun and made darkness. Their thin, large wings gleamed and glittered. The rasping whirring of their wings filled the whole air and they hit the ground and the house with the noise of a hailstorm."*

Farms on the Great Plains were again devastated by nature in the 1930s. Find out about the drought called the "Dust Bowl" and how it affected farm families.

Science makes little distinction between locusts and grasshoppers. They are different names for the same insect. A locust is a grasshopper in its migrating phase, its swarming phase. A grasshopper's body chemistry changes, and it becomes a locust.

THE TRAIN HOLD-UP

The Rocky Mountain locust plagued early settlers on America's Great Plains. Outbreaks in 1855, 1864, and 1866 destroyed farms and sent homesteaders trudging back east. The 1874 swarm, 1,800 miles long and 110 miles wide, devastated lives from Canada to Texas. Young Laura Ingalls was not the only homesteader with memories of that swarm. A Kansas woman named Mary Lyon recalled how, on August 1, "There was a haze in the air and the sun was veiled:

> *"They began, toward night, dropping to the earth.... They devoured every green thing but the prairie grass.... I thought to save some of my garden by covering it with gunny sacks, but the hoppers regarded that as a huge joke and...ate their way through."*

The locusts ate gardens and orchards. They ate wooden tool handles and leather harnesses. They ate clothes and curtains. They ate dead animals and sheep wool. When they landed on railroad tracks, they made them so slippery that the trains couldn't move.

Then they moved on. By 1878, the locusts were gone—never to swarm again. The last specimens of the Rocky Mountain locust were collected in Canada in 1902. The species was declared extinct.

No one is sure what did in the Rocky Mountain locust. Most scientists agree that loss of habitat was responsible. Farmers plowed up the damp regions near western streams that were the insect's natural breeding grounds. But there is no real evidence. A few scientists believe that the species is not extinct at all but only went back to its normal, grasshopper phase. If that's so, it may only be a matter of time before its chemistry changes again.

What feature of "Grasshoppers Gone Wild" is *not* found in "Desert Swarm"?

   A   visual aids

   B   scientific data

   C   dates of outbreaks

   D   eyewitness accounts

> Both of these articles give information about the same topic. They both include visual aids, scientific data about locusts, and dates of outbreaks. Only the second article, though, includes accounts by people who actually experienced locust swarms. That lets Peter Minner's article "place you there" in a way that Abbas Samhadi's article doesn't. Choice D is the correct answer.

What does the photo in "Grasshoppers Gone Wild" show?

_____

_____

_____

> The photo, obviously fake, illustrates a fact about the locust swarm in a humorous way. It shows a locust "holding up" a train, but the question is asking for more than a literal answer. Here is a sample answer:

> The picture is a kind of joke. The article describes how grasshoppers on railroad tracks kept trains from moving. If the picture is from the time of the great locust swarm, it shows that people could find ways to laugh about it.

What is similar and what is different between the desert locust and the Rocky Mountain locust?

_____

_____

_____

_____

_____

_____

_____

✓ This question asks you to compare and contrast information from both sources. Here is one possible answer:

Both insects are usually not a problem, but changes in their chemistry cause them to breed, swarm, and eat out of control. When that happens, they can ruin farms over wide areas. They can travel hundreds of miles. The Rocky Mountain locust may form bigger swarms, but the desert locust can cover wider areas. It can cross oceans, while the Rocky Mountain locust stays in the U.S. and Canada. The desert locust is still a problem, but the Rocky Mountain locust is probably extinct.

Which of these items of information is found in "Grasshoppers Gone Wild" but *not* in "Desert Swarm"?

A   Locusts fly with the wind.

B   Locusts, when swarming, eat almost any kind of plant.

C   Locusts and grasshoppers are basically the same insect.

D   The Rocky Mountain locust caused enormous crop damage in the United States.

> When you get information from more than one source, certain items will be repeated while others will be found only in a particular source. Only in Samhadi's article will you learn that locusts fly with the wind. Information on what they eat and on the damage caused by the Rocky Mountain locust is found in both articles. Only Minner tells you that *grasshopper* and *locust* are different names for the same insect. Choice C is the correct answer.

List four facts that you might include in a report on locust swarms. Include items from both articles and from the visual aids.

_____

_____

_____

_____

> If you were writing a report on the topic, you would combine information from several sources. Putting information together from several sources, including both text and visual elements, can help you answer a question or solve a problem more effectively than information from one source alone. Here are a few possible items you might include:

1—Having abundant food causes grasshoppers' body chemistry to change.

2—The desert locust ruined wide areas of Africa in 2003–2005.

3—There were desert locust outbreaks almost every year from 1940 to 1963.

4—The Rocky Mountain locust used to be as big a problem as the desert locust.

Visual elements can also add to the meaning or tone of a literary text. Think about the picture books you read as a young child, or the illustrated literature you may still read today—even "graphic stories" such as those found in comic books and graphic novels. An example is the following passage. It comes from a graphic version of a traditional tale told by the Choctaw, an American Indian people.

Guided Practice

Read the passage. Then answer the questions.

from **Rabbit's Choctaw Tail Tale**

adapted by Tim Tingle, illustrated by Pat Lewis

Explain how the illustrations help you to better understand these elements of the story:

Characters _____

_____

_____

Events _____

_____

_____

Setting _____

_____

_____

Tone _____

_____

_____

✓ Read the excerpt again, but try not to pay attention to the illustrations. It's hard to do, isn't it? Can you see how the illustrations add to your appreciation of all the elements of the narrative? Here are some sample answers:

Characters—The illustrations show that Rabbit is a silly character, while Fox is more serious. Rabbit always has a stupid grin, while Fox looks happy, angry, or thoughtful.

Events—The illustrations help move the story along. In the first two illustrations, you can see Rabbit smelling the fish that Fox caught, even though he's far away. The later illustrations show the different ways that Fox is responding to Rabbit, who is trying to get Fox to give him the fish.

Setting—With illustrations, you don't need the author to describe the setting. You can see that it's a hilly country with woods and rocks.

Tone—The illustrator chose a cartoon style for the illustrations. They create a funny, happy tone. It tells you that the story is meant to make you laugh. No one in this story is really going to get hurt.

Test Yourself

Passage 1

In the Canyonlands, the sun is the unquestioned king, and I his humble subject. Other people might choose to experience nature in dark woods, on the slopes of snowy mountains, or beside gurgling streams. I prefer the harsh majesty of the desert. Here the tallest plants are mesquite bushes, and the streams, where you can find them, don't gurgle—they roar.

I discovered Canyonlands National Park on a college vacation. My buddies and I made the trek to the Grand Canyon in an ill-tempered Volkswagen bus. The canyon was breathtaking, but the crowds were smothering. I decided then that a trail as noisy and congested as a shopping mall was not what you could call "nature." But the map showed another national park upstream in Utah, and that was where we headed next.

In the Canyonlands was where I first heard silence. It was late afternoon. As I gazed at those spires and arches shaped by wind and flood, I saw a hundred shades of red. It was so still that I could hear the rustle of a whiptail lizard and the beating wings of a horned lark. The rattlesnakes seemed as sleepy and content as house cats. There was not another human being in sight. And this was at The Needles, the most popular part of the park. To speak amid such splendor, even to whisper, would have been like shouting in church.

You can access most regions of the park with an all-wheel drive vehicle on dirt roads. But it's better to experience it by hiking trail, or by running Cataract Canyon on a raft. If you have the equipment and experience, the park's finest adventures are to be found on the off-trail routes. There are more than these than you can explore in a lifetime. Take it from someone who's tried.

spires
tall, slender objects that taper to a point, like a church steeple

Passage 2

The Colorado and Green Rivers divide the Canyonlands into a gigantic Y. In the middle, Island in the Sky Mesa stands 2,000 feet above the rivers. East of the Colorado stand the rock spires of The Needles and the arches, ruins, and prehistoric Native Indian rock art of Salt Creek. West of the rivers is The Maze, the least-visited part of the park. Running between them are the rivers themselves, including Cataract Canyon with its 24 rapids.

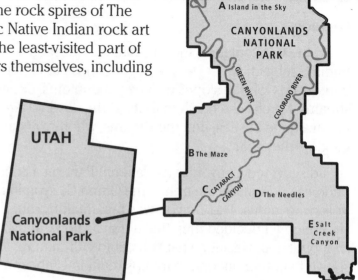

1 In passage 1, which of these sentences is *best* illustrated by the photograph?

A In the Canyonlands, the sun is the unquestioned king, and I his humble subject.

B As I gazed at those spires and arches shaped by wind and flood, I saw a hundred shades of red.

C Here the tallest plants are mesquite bushes, and the streams, where you can find them, don't gurgle—they roar.

D If you have the equipment and experience, the park's finest adventures are to be found on the off-trail routes.

2 How does the photograph help you understand the feelings the author expresses about Canyonlands National Park?

_____

_____

_____

_____

_____

3 What is the purpose of the two maps included with passage 2?

_____

_____

_____

_____

_____

4 Which area on the map of the park is the *most* popular?

   A A

   B B

   C C

   D D

5 What form of transportation would be *most* useful in the area marked C on the map?

   A a raft

   B a horse

   C your feet

   D an off-road vehicle

6 Which area shown on the map of the park do you think the author of passage 1 likes *best* to visit? Explain why?

_____

_____

_____

_____

_____

UNIT 4
Integration of Knowledge and Ideas

Identifying Connections

RI.5.8

Vocabulary

discipline

enforcing

When you read for information, you know you are reading facts—or do you? If an author doesn't offer evidence for the points she is making, you may not be reading facts at all. You may be reading the author's opinions.

What's the difference? A **fact** is a statement that can be proven. An **opinion** tells you how the author, or someone else, thinks and feels about a subject. Judgmental words like *best* or *worst* can show that someone is expressing an opinion, not a fact. So can generalizations that use words like *everyone, nobody, always,* or *never.*

In some texts, such as newspaper editorials, Internet blogs, and critical reviews of books, movies, or restaurants, you know the author is expressing opinions that support the purpose of persuading readers to his point of view. But does he support his opinions with reasons? If not, you're reading a rant, not an editorial.

As you read, pay attention to the points the author makes. Are facts backed up with evidence? Facts from a firsthand source, such as an eyewitness, are usually more accurate than secondhand information. Does the source know what she's talking about? Is she an expert, or is she just "spouting off"? Are you reading complete information, or is the author leaving out facts that don't support his opinions? Is the information up-to-date, or are you reading old "facts" that time has turned into fiction? Does the author clearly favor one side of an argument even though she pretends to be fair and balanced in her opinions? Asking yourself questions like these when you read for information will help you separate fact from fantasy—and maybe truth from lies!

Guided Practice

Read the passage. Then answer the questions.

⭐ Welcome to Internet — □ X

File   Edit   View   Favorites   Tools   Help

◁ ▷ ↻ 🏠   www.janespage.com

Jane's Page

News and Musings About the Environment

by Jane Page

Do you believe that trees should be a product of nature? I do! That's why I'm worried about the genetically altered eucalyptus trees that are soon to be planted in our country.

A company called ArborGen has developed the new trees for three large paper companies. In May 2010, they got approval from the United States Department of Agriculture to do test plantings. Up to 250,000 trees will be planted in sites in seven states, covering about 300 acres.

Eucalyptus trees are native to Australia. They grow fast and produce pulp that is perfect for making paper. But they require a hot climate. ArborGen has altered the genes of eucalyptus so that they can survive in freezing temperatures. The company claims that their trees can help preserve forests by producing more wood in less space. The government says they're safe for the environment. However, not enough testing has been done to support either claim.

Eucalyptus trees are not native to the United States. In other cases where non-native species have been introduced, they have caused environmental disaster. The mongoose, for example, has all but wiped out native birds in Hawaii. The zebra mussel has clogged drainpipes and infested lakes and rivers over much of our country. And every Southerner knows what happened after the kudzu vine was introduced in the 1870s.

In parts of California, *natural* eucalyptus trees were introduced in the 1850s. They have crowded out native oak forests, wiping out animal species that need oaks for food and habitat. They soak up huge amounts of water that is needed for drinking and farming. Their leaves and litter contain oils that easily spread fires. The destructive Oakland Hills fire of 1991 was largely fueled by eucalyptus trees.

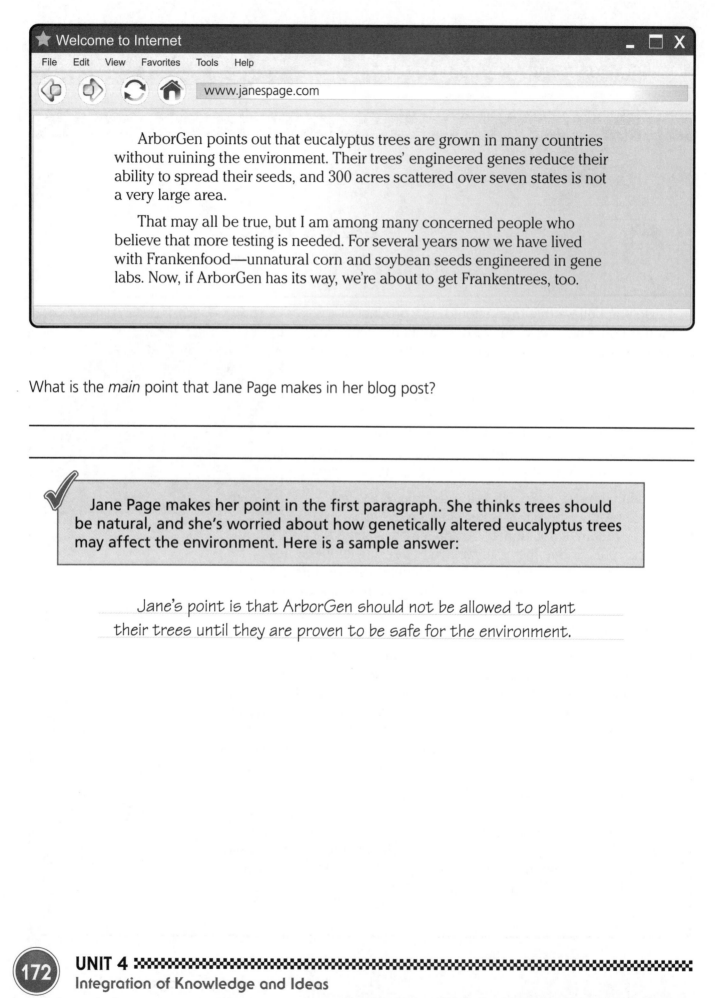

Welcome to Internet

File　Edit　View　Favorites　Tools　Help

www.janespage.com

ArborGen points out that eucalyptus trees are grown in many countries without ruining the environment. Their trees' engineered genes reduce their ability to spread their seeds, and 300 acres scattered over seven states is not a very large area.

That may all be true, but I am among many concerned people who believe that more testing is needed. For several years now we have lived with Frankenfood—unnatural corn and soybean seeds engineered in gene labs. Now, if ArborGen has its way, we're about to get Frankentrees, too.

What is the *main* point that Jane Page makes in her blog post?

_____

_____

✓ Jane Page makes her point in the first paragraph. She thinks trees should be natural, and she's worried about how genetically altered eucalyptus trees may affect the environment. Here is a sample answer:

Jane's point is that ArborGen should not be allowed to plant their trees until they are proven to be safe for the environment.

Which of these ideas from paragraph 3 is an opinion?

A Eucalyptus wood is just right for making paper.

B Not enough testing has been done on the altered trees.

C The government says the altered trees are safe for the environment.

D ArborGen has altered eucalyptus genes so that they can survive freezing temperatures.

What's "enough"? You can assume that *some* testing has been done, or the Department of Agriculture wouldn't have approved the trees. With some research, you could confirm that eucalyptus wood is ideal for making paper. You could find the government's report on the test results, and altering the genes so that they could survive in cold temperatures was the very point of the project. Some experts have said that the tests were adequate. Others might believe that no amount of testing would be "enough." Choice B is the correct answer.

What are two reasons Jane Page uses to support her argument? What evidence does she offer to support each reason?

_____

_____

_____

_____

_____

_____

Jane has solid reasons for her opinions. Here is one way to answer the question:

She says that introducing new species to an environment is a bad idea. As evidence, she mentions species that have caused environmental disasters, like the mongoose and the zebra mussel. She says that eucalyptus trees harm the environment. Her evidence is that they have crowded out native oak trees in California and contain an oil that can cause forest fires.

Does Jane Page present both sides of the argument? Explain why, or why not.

_____

_____

 Jane has her opinions, but she does not completely ignore opinions on the other side. Here is one possible answer:

Yes, because paragraph 6 states several reasons that ArborGen says their trees are safe.

Do you think Jane Page's closing paragraph is convincing? Explain why, or why not.

_____

_____

_____

_____

For the most part in her blog, Jane presents a reasoned argument. The last paragraph, however, is maybe not so reasoned. Here is one possible answer:

No, because it's a weak argument that relies on scary words like "Frankenfood" and "Frankentrees" instead of evidence. She makes the genetically altered plants sound like monsters, but she doesn't say whether they have proven to be bad for people or for the environment.

Test Yourself

Read the passage. Then answer the questions.

Dear Editor,

I'm a fifth grader at Moody Elementary School. I would like to nominate my teacher, Mr. Patrick Barnes, for your newspaper's Teacher of the Year award.

Mr. Barnes came into our classroom at the end of November. Until then, we had had a series of substitutes since the start of school. None of them stayed longer than two weeks. Kids can't learn anything without a full-time teacher.

Mr. Barnes took control of our class right away. He made it clear that discipline would be tough but fair. He posted his rules and started enforcing them the first day. Anyone who broke a rule more than once quickly learned that he meant what he said. The noise level in the classroom dropped to almost nothing. That made it easier to learn.

Mr. Barnes also showed that he cared about us. He knew everyone's name by the second day. He was always willing to spend time with us as individuals. He quickly noticed that math was my worst subject. He took me aside and talked to me about the problem I was having. He directed me to a website that he thought would help me understand it better. When I told him we didn't have a computer at home, he made sure I was able to use one in the library. My math scores started improving right away. When I got an "A" at the end of the semester, he wrote "Good for you!" on my report sheet.

We worked hard in his class, but we had fun, too. When we were studying history, we had a class debate on the Boston Tea Party. Mr. Barnes offered extra credit to anyone who came dressed in a costume from the Revolutionary War period. Even a homemade wig and a hat counted. He also told us stories about his army service in the Iraq War. That was to help us understand something about a soldier's life. I think Mr. Barnes was a real hero.

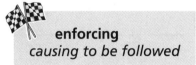

discipline
trained condition of order and obedience

enforcing
causing to be followed

Then there was "Culture Day," March 12. Some kids in our class came from other countries. A few of them still hadn't learned English very well. Mr. Barnes made everyone feel like they belonged. He had us all talk a little about where we came from and bring some special food to share. Those of us who were born here in the USA celebrated our own family's culture, too. It made everyone feel special about being Americans and being ourselves, too.

Even our parents and the other teachers think Mr. Barnes is special. I know there are a lot of fine teachers in our city, but I bet there's none better than Mr. Barnes. I think he is well deserving of your Teacher of the Year award.

Sincerely,
Luke

1 What is the *main* point of Luke's argument?

_____

_____

_____

_____

_____

2 What are *three* reasons Luke gives in support of his argument, and the evidence for each?

Reason A: _____

_____

Reason B: _____

_____

Reason C: _____

_____

UNIT 4 ▰▰▰▰▰▰▰▰▰▰▰▰▰▰▰▰▰▰▰▰▰▰▰▰▰▰▰▰▰▰▰
Integration of Knowledge and Ideas

3 Which of these sentences states an opinion?

    A Mr. Barnes came into our classroom at the end of November.

    B Until then, we had had a series of substitutes since the start of school.

    C None of them stayed longer than two weeks.

    D Kids can't learn anything without a full-time teacher.

4 Which of these sentences states a fact?

    A We worked hard in his class, but we had fun, too.

    B Some kids in our class came from other countries.

    C Mr. Barnes made everyone feel like they belonged.

    D It made everyone feel special about being Americans and being ourselves, too.

5 What is a point Luke makes that is *not* supported by reasons and evidence? Explain your answer.

_____

_____

_____

_____

_____

Comparing and Contrasting

RL.5.9

Vocabulary
ajar
ballistics
courageous
vandalism

What's your favorite genre to read? **Genre** (ZHON•ruh) is a word that means a particular kind or style of literature. Science fiction is a familiar example of a genre. When you're reading a story set on another planet or that involves time travel, you can identify it immediately as science fiction, even though the space alien characters, seem like real people.

Books in a particular genre have elements that are similar to one another, but there is a lot of variety, too. Consider for example Natalie Babbitt's *Tuck Everlasting* and Susan Cooper's *The Dark is Rising* series. They are both fantasies. They are both set in our world and involve characters who cannot die. That's where the similarities end. The characters, events, settings, and especially the tone of the books are completely different.

Genres and the differences among and within them add variety and spice to your reading. **Realistic fiction** is probably what you read most often. It is usually about people who could be real. Many authors write stories specifically about situations that modern people face. Books by writers such as Virginia Hamilton and Christopher Paul Curtis are realistic modern fiction.

Historical fiction can also be realistic, but it takes place in a different time period. The characters in historical fiction are facing similar challenges to those in realistic fiction, but in a very different setting—colonial America or ancient Rome, for example.

Science fiction and **fantasies** are stories that take place in unreal settings or that feature unreal events. A science fiction story may have nonhuman characters or people living far in the future. Usually some element of science fact forms the background to the story. A fantasy, by contrast, may feature humans with extraordinary powers, imaginary worlds that are something like ours but in which magic is real, or fantastic creatures such as unicorns or vampires.

Traditional literature includes several genres of stories that people have told since before writing was invented. A **myth** may try to explain something about nature or a people's customs or beliefs. Some of the best-known myths are those of the ancient Greeks and Romans. A **legend,** like the stories of Robin Hood, is a tale from the past about people and events. It is usually connected to a particular time or place. A **folktale** is a story of ordinary people that contains a lesson about human behavior. A **fable** is a very short folktale in which the characters may be animals portrayed as human types. A **fairy tale** is involves magical creatures, such as fairies or witches, interacting with human beings in good and wicked ways.

Any kind of narrative may be identified as belonging to a literary genre, even some forms of nonfiction. A **biography,** for example, is a narrative of a person's life. An **autobiography** is a biography written by the subject herself. A **personal essay** describes and reflects upon something that is important to the author's life. When you recognize the genre of what you are reading, you can understand better where an author is taking you and how he means for you to enjoy his work.

Guided Practice

Read two passages. Then answer the questions.

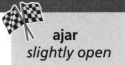

ajar
slightly open

from **Detectives with Backpacks**

by Shandra White

It was Jason's fault that she was late. Her brother seemed to take longer in the bathroom every day. That was something to take up at a family meeting. Katrina was glad for her soccer training as she ran the last block to school, although she never played soccer while wearing a backpack full of books. The five-minute bell had rung, and kids were filing into the building. Katrina hated being late for anything, even school. You never know what you might miss, and she was proud of her perfect attendance record.

A knot of kids was talking excitedly in front of Room 114. The classroom door was ajar, but here were Monica and Henry and the Hazewood twins and two or three others all jabbering at once. Katrina heard the words "police" and "stolen" before Emma Hazewood half-turned and saw her.

"Katrina, have you heard?"

"Heard what?"

Six kids started talking, but it was Monica Peters, a head taller than anyone else, who broke in and said, "Shut up, all of you. Let me tell it." She was excited and out of breath. "The police were just here, and they took Mr. Dabney away."

"Mr. Dabney the custodian?" Katrina wasn't sure she had heard Monica correctly. "Mr. Dabney" and "police" hardly belonged in the same sentence together.

"You know any other Mr. Dabney?" Monica said. "You know the money the PTA raised to pay for new band instruments? Well, Mr. Dabney stole it."

"Oh, come on, Monica! You don't know that!" Henry Campbell said.

"'Innocent until proven guilty.'"

"Oh, right, Emma," Monica said. "They found the envelope in his broom closet and a big wad of cash in his wallet. And maybe you don't know this," she added importantly to Katrina, "but my mom told me that Mr. Dabney has been in trouble with the police before!"

"That still isn't proof of anything," Henry objected, but just then the door opened fully and Ms. Vetzner stood there with her stern face on.

"Class it's nine o'clock. And maybe you don't know *this,*" she said, with a look at Monica, "but a wise man once called gossip 'the evil tongue.'" The teacher made sure she made eye contact with everyone. "Now, let's get started on our work for today, and we'll let the police do theirs."

Still talking, the kids filed into class. Katrina hung back, last in line. She was thinking of the first grade, when she was always leaving her jacket or a book or something behind in class. Mr. Dabney had seemed like a giant from a fairy tale to her then, monstrous and slow-moving and a little scary. When he frowned and said, "Oh, Katrina, not again!" he might as well have been saying "fee-fie-fo-fum." But he was really very kind. He would joke and chat with her dad as he unlocked the classroom door for her, and he would always leave her with a smile. Everyone liked Mr. Dabney. Katrina couldn't imagine him being a thief.

"That's impossible!" she murmured aloud, entering the classroom just before Ms. Vetzner shut the door behind her.

from **That Great Day of Anger**

by Simon Peerce

"This is Rios."

"Detective Lieutenant Rios?"

The guy's voice on the phone sounded like he was talking through 40 years of cigar smoke. "That's me."

"This is Detective Lieutenant Zarnecki, Chicago homicide."

"Oh," I said, suddenly alert. "Thanks for getting back to me, Lieutenant."

"Interesting case you've got out there on the coast," Zarnecki growled.

I waited for him to continue. Then I realized he was enjoying my wait. "You've got something for me?" I pressed.

"We ran a background check on your victim," Zarnecki said. "Turns out Dr. Lawrence Friedman did have a police record, but only as a juvenile. Got mixed up with a gang called the Jokers."

"What kind of stuff was he involved in?"

UNIT 4
Integration of Knowledge and Ideas

"Well, it was juvie, so the records are sealed. But the Jokers were never into really bad stuff. Some vandalism and petty violence, but no guns, no drug dealing. Nothing to keep Friedman out of medical school once he straightened himself out."

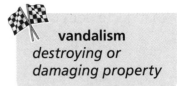

vandalism
destroying or damaging property

There was a pause on the line. I could hear the Chicago detective breathing into the phone. I was a fish, and he was playing me on the line.

"Detective Zarnecki, do I detect a 'but' in that silence?"

"Yeah, well, here's the interesting part. We ran a computer search on your ballistics report. We do that routinely here, as I'm sure you do, to see if the weapon was used in any other crimes on record."

ballistics
a scientific test used by police to determine from which gun a shot was fired

I found I was gripping the phone like it was my last dollar. "And?"

"Well, turns out it was. An old man name of Speaker was shot with that very same gun. A retired high-school gym teacher. Lived alone. Answered a knock at his door, and boom."

"You're going to tell me that your victim was a teacher at the school where our victim was involved in gang activity?"

"Wish I could. Different school entirely. Miles away on the other side of town. But, here's the thing. Speaker was shot about nine o'clock on the evening of Wednesday, April 9."

That took a moment to sink in. "Friedman was shot at 5:30 a.m. on April 10," I said slowly.

"So your report said," Zarnecki said with apparent satisfaction.

"You're telling me our bad guy got Speaker in Chicago Wednesday night, hopped on a plane, and got to Los Angeles in time to shoot Friedman walking his dog the next morning?"

"That's what it looks like."

"Well, it's just possible. How did he get a gun through airport security?"

"Good question, isn't it? I can't get a tube of toothpaste through that line without making bells ring. I've got my people at O'Hare Airport working on it right now."

What genre does both of these selections belong to?

A mystery

B science fiction

C historical fiction

D traditional literature

✓ The word "detectives" in the title of the first passage may have tipped you off before you even began reading it. Both of these selections seem to be set in the present day, or at least in recent time. They involve real people in real settings, not space aliens or talking animals with human characteristics. You probably recognized elements of both passages as characteristic of a mystery. Choice A is the correct answer.

What are three elements that the two stories have in common?

_____

_____

_____

✓ Stories about crime and punishment go back at least as far as the ancient Egyptians. But a mystery involves more than seeing a "bad guy" get what's coming to him. Here is one sample answer:

Both stories involve a crime or crimes. Both stories involve a puzzle, in which readers try to figure out "whodunit?" Both stories feature a detective character who is trying to solve the puzzle.

What are three elements that are different between these stories?

_____

_____

_____

_____

_____

_____

_____

All mysteries involve a crime, a puzzle, and a detective. Beyond that, there are many differences among them. There are "police procedurals," in which readers follow police officers in their gritty and painstaking detail work. There are "hard-boiled" detective stories, featuring a tough, honest "private eye" who frequently finds himself in danger. There are "English drawing-room" mysteries, in which an elegant detective solves a difficult puzzle without getting his white gloves dirty. The two passages you've just read are as different as two stories in the same genre can be. One is evidently aimed at young readers, while the other is intended for adults. Here is a sample answer:

The scene from "Detectives with Backpacks" is set in an elementary school. The scene from "That Great Day of Anger" is set in a big-city police station. You can guess from the title that the "detectives with backpacks" are Katrina and her friends, while Rios in the second story is a real police detective. The narrator in "Backpacks" uses plain language, while Detective Rios in "Anger" uses colorful metaphors and similes, like "gripping the phone like it was my last dollar."

Predict what will happen as the two stories continue.

_____

_____

_____

_____

_____

_____

 It's hard to make a prediction from such short excerpts, but you can make some good guesses based on your knowledge of the mystery genre. Here is one way to answer the question:

In both stories, the puzzle will be solved. Katrina and her friends will prove Mr. Dabney to be innocent. Since the story is meant for kids, there probably won't be any real danger or violence. Detective Rios will try to connect the murder in his city with the one in Chicago to figure out who did it. There will probably be something exciting like a chase or a shoot-out.

UNIT 4 ░░░
Integration of Knowledge and Ideas

Test Yourself

Tess and the Sparrow

by Colton Roberts Jr.

Once in late autumn, I was on my way home after a long day of hunting. I was walking toward my house along a forest path. My dog Tess was with me, running a little way ahead. A strong wind had come up, and I was tired and glad to be going home.

Suddenly, Tess stopped short and lifted her nose into the air. She sniffed in one direction, and again in another. Then she crouched and began to creep forward, as though she had caught the scent of game.

I peered up the path ahead of me and saw a young sparrow. The wind was making the birch trees sway, and apparently the tiny bird had fallen from its nest. Now it stood in the middle of the path, trying to use its barely grown wings to fly away.

My dog had barely reached the infant sparrow when, suddenly, an older bird landed right in front of Tess's face. With all her feathers standing straight on end, she gave a courageous chirp and hopped once and then again toward Tess's open mouth.

courageous
brave

The bird had thrown herself in front of the dog to protect her offspring. Yet her own small body was trembling with terror and her little voice sounded frightened. Tess must have looked like a monster to her. However, the mother sparrow couldn't bear to remain safe in the tree. A feeling that was stronger than her will to survive made her hurry to the rescue.

Tess stopped still and then retreated. Maybe she understood the mother bird's instinct. I called her to my side and, with a final glance at the two birds, we returned to our house by a different path.

All evening I was in awe of that mother bird. I learned from her that love is sometimes stronger than the fear of death.

1 Which of the following would describe both "Tess and the Sparrow" and "The Revenge of Albus"?

A fable

B realistic fiction

C personal essay

D autobiography

2 Explain your answer to question 1.

_____

_____

_____

_____

3 Which of these elements of a narrative is *most* similar between the
two passages?

A tone

B theme

C setting

D events

4 Explain your answer to question 3.

_____

_____

_____

_____

5 What is similar and what is different about the way the authors write
about their topic?

_____

_____

_____

_____

_____

REVIEW

Integration of Knowledge and Ideas

Vocabulary
palatable
pioneer

Read two passages. Then answer the questions.

The Snake

a tale from West Africa

One cold winter day, a woman was walking home along a lonely country road. Suddenly, she heard a soft hissing sound. She looked and saw a cobra trapped between two rocks.

"Lady, please help me," the snake hissed. "I'm cold, I'm hungry, and I'm trapped here. If you don't help me, I'll die." The woman felt sorry for the poor serpent. She carefully moved the rocks and freed it.

"Thank you," said the snake. "Now, won't you please take me home with you? All I need is some food and a warm place to spend the night, and I'll be on my way in the morning."

The kindhearted woman carried the snake home, warming it with her hands. She lit a fire in her stove and gave the snake some food. Soon it was fit and healthy and slithering about the floor of her house.

The woman sat down in her chair and held the snake on her lap. The snake sprang up and bit her savagely.

"Oh!" cried the woman. "How could you do such a thing? I saved your life! I took you in and fed you, and now I may die from your poisonous bite!"

"Lady," the serpent hissed, "I'm a snake. Didn't you know that before you took me in?"

Nasreddin Hodja and the Walnut Tree

a tale from Turkey

The tales of Nasreddin Hodja are known throughout the Middle East. They may be based on the life and teachings of a real imam (Muslim religious teacher) of the 1200s.

In all the world, was there ever a wiser judge than Nasreddin Hodja? From his day unto ours are his noble decisions and wise pronouncements known!

One day, Nasreddin Hodja was resting in the shade of an old walnut tree. As befits a judge and teacher, the Hodja's mind was busy even as his body was at rest. He mused, "Was it wise for such a big tree to bear such tiny fruit? Behold its great trunk and sturdy branches! Consider the pumpkins in the field beyond that wall. They grow on scrawny vines that can't even support their own weight. Why did the walnuts not grow on vines and pumpkins on mighty trees?"

No sooner had the Hodja's eyes closed for his nap than a walnut fell from the tree and struck him on the forehead. He woke up, startled, and exclaimed, "Praise be! If the world had been created according to my poor understanding, it would have been a pumpkin that hit me on the head and surely have killed me!"

And never again did Nasreddin Hodja question the wisdom of Nature.

1 "The Snake" should *probably* be considered to be a _____.

A fable

B myth

C legend

D fairy tale

2 "Nasreddin Hodja and the Walnut Tree" should *probably* be considered to be a _____.

A fable

B myth

C legend

D fairy tale

3 Explain your answers to questions 1 and 2.

_____

_____

_____

_____

_____

4 How do the illustrations contribute to your understanding and appreciation of the stories?

_____

_____

_____

_____

_____

5 What is similar and what is different between "The Snake" and the excerpt from "Rabbit's Choctaw Tail Tale" on pages 164–165?

_____

_____

_____

_____

_____

6 What is similar and what is different between "Nasreddin Hodja and the Walnut Tree" and the story "Justice" on pages 97–98?

_____

_____

_____

_____

_____

Independence Rock: the "Register of the Desert"

by Edward Miller

Independence Rock stands above the high plains of Wyoming not far from the Sweetwater River. It's a rounded granite hill, rising about 120 feet high above the patchy dry grass. If not for the signs, travelers on State Highway 220 might not know that they were looking at history.

Independence Rock marked the halfway point of the famous Oregon Trail. Wagon trains of the years 1843–1869 made it their goal to reach this landmark by July 4. If they did, they would likely avoid autumn snow in the mountains farther west. Legend has it that that's how the rock got its name. In fact, it was called Independence Rock as early as the 1820s, when a group of fur trappers celebrated Independence Day there.

Still, reaching the rock on the Fourth was a cause for celebration, as many pioneer diaries attest. As Margaret Hecox wrote, "Being the Fourth of July, we concluded to lay by and celebrate the day. The children had no fireworks, but we all joined in singing patriotic songs and shared in a picnic lunch." James Nesmith commented, "Had the pleasure of waiting on five or six young ladies to pay a visit to Independence Rock. I had the satisfaction of putting the names of Miss Mary Zachary and Miss Jane Mills on the southeast point of the rocks."

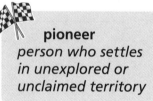

pioneer
person who settles in unexplored or unclaimed territory

It's an easy climb to the top of Independence Rock. From there you can see the prairie, the mountains, and the westward course of the Sweetwater much as the pioneers saw them. Like Mary Zachary and Jane Mills, many of them left their names and other messages on the rock. About five thousand of them are still visible today, carved with chisels or written in axle grease.

from Journal of a Trip to Oregon in 1852

by Abigail Jane Scott

June 29—We came twenty miles. We struck the Sweet water about two o'clock and about three came to Independence rock; The Sweet water is about one hundred feet in width; The water is clear and palatable but is warmer during the day than water of the Platte.

Independence rock is an immense mass covering an area of, I think about ten acres, and is about three hundred feet high; My sisters and I went to the base of the rock with the intention of climbing it but we had only ascended about thirty feet when a heavy hail and wind storm arose obliging us to desist; We then started on after the wagons and before we reached them they had all crossed the river except the last to overtake. They had intended to let us wade it (it was waist deep) to learn us not to get so far behind the team; I would have liked the fun of wading well enough but did not like to get joked about being left. Immediately after leaving Independence rock we came in sight of the well known Devil's Gate five miles ahead of us and when we came near enough we turned off the road about one mile and halted for the night opposite to it in a bend of the river.

We in company with many others paid this gate a visit; It is indeed a sight worth seeing; The Sweet water passes through it, and it really seems left by providence for the river to pass through as we can see no other place where it can find its way through the rocks; The cliffs of rock on either side are at least four hundred feet in height and on the South side almost perfectly perpendicular; The rocks are in many places covered with names of visitors to this place a few of which were of as early date as '38 a great many were dated '50 and '51 but the majority were '52. We passed seven graves.

palatable
food that is agreeable enough to be eaten

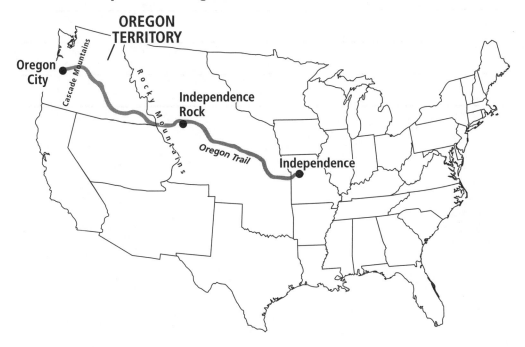

Integration of Knowledge and Ideas

7 Which of these statements in Edward Miller's article is an opinion?

   A It's an easy climb to the top of Independence Rock.

   B About five thousand of them are still visible on the rock today.

   C Wagon trains of the years 1843–1869 made it their goal to reach this landmark by July 4.

   D Independence Rock stands above the high plains of Wyoming not far from the Sweetwater River.

8 Which of these statements in Miller's article is supported by the map?

   A Independence Rock marked the halfway point of the famous Oregon Trail.

   B It's a rounded granite hill, rising about 120 feet high above the patchy dry grass.

   C If not for the signs, travelers on State Highway 220 might not know that they were looking at history.

   D From there you can see the prairie, the mountains, and the westward course of the Sweetwater much as the pioneers saw them.

9 What evidence does Miller give to support his point that the wagon-train pioneers did *not* name Independence Rock?

_____

_____

_____

_____

_____

UNIT 4 ▪▪
Integration of Knowledge and Ideas

10 Read this sentence from "Independence Rock."

*Still, reaching the rock on the Fourth was a cause for celebration,
as many pioneer diaries attest.*

Do you think his evidence for this statement supports this point?
Explain why, or why not.

_____

_____

_____

_____

_____

11 Does Abigail Jane Scott's diary entry support the points Miller makes
in his article?

_____

_____

_____

_____

_____

12 How does Scott's journal entry help you to better understand the
information in Miller's article?

_____

_____

_____

_____

_____

13 Miller gives the height of Independence Rock as 120 feet, Scott as 300 feet. Whose figure do you think is more accurate? Explain why.

_____

_____

_____

_____

_____

14 How do the two photographs help you to better understand _both_ the article and the diary entry?

_____

_____

_____

_____

_____

PRACTICE TEST

Vocabulary

bouquet
docile
omnipotent
prodigious
rebellion
succulent
supercilious

Read two poems. Then answer the questions.

I Like to See It Lap the Miles

by Emily Dickinson

I like to see it lap the miles
And lick the valleys up,
And stop to feed itself at tanks;
And then—prodigious[1] step

5   Around a pile of mountains,
And, supercilious,[2] peer
In shanties by the side of roads;
And then a quarry pare

To fit its sides and crawl between,
10 Complaining all the while
In horrid, hooting stanza;
Then chase itself down hill—
And neigh like Boanerges;
Then, prompter than a star

15 Stop—docile[3] and omnipotent,[4]
At its own stable door—

---

[1]**prodigious:** huge

[2]**supercilious:** proud and scornful

[3]**docile:** gentle

[4]**omnipotent:** all-powerful

The Runaway Engine

Anonymous

Once there was a little engine who was full of discontent.
He didn't like the work he did or the journey he was sent.
And he grumbled to himself as he puffed his way uphill,
"I think it's time I had a change; I really feel quite ill."

5   "I've had enough of trucks of coal and nasty smelly fish,
And to have a more important job is the one thing that I wish,
And just because I'm little they don't listen when I speak,
But I'll make them hear me this time if it takes me all week."

So he snorted and he blew, and he made a lot of din,
10   But not the slightest notice did his driver take of him.
This so annoyed the engine that with rage he really shook,
And then he gave his driver a nasty, horrid look.

"I'll teach him not to listen," he stuttered through his steam.
He stamped his wheels with temper and really made a scene.
15   "I won't put up with this," he said, "another single day!
There's only one thing left to do—I'll have to run away."

So that night when none could see him, he crept out of his shed,
And tired of going uphill went the other way instead.
"Now this is rather fun," he said, and gave a little hop,
20   But he soon found to his horror that he simply couldn't stop.

Faster, faster went his wheels, his whistle blew with fright.
He went so fast he left the rails—how he wished that he could stop,
But he went right in the water with a simply frightful plop!

He lay there and he gurgled for he couldn't even shout,
25   And he said that he was sorry when they came and pulled him out.
And now he whistles gaily as he does his work each day,
For he knows he'd rather stay at home than ever run away.

1 In "I Like to See It Lap the Miles," what metaphor does Dickinson use to describe the train?

   A   a giant

   B   a horse

   C   a queen

   D   a warrior

2 In "The Runaway Engine," what metaphor does the poet use to describe the engine?

   A   a car

   B   a child

   C   a dragon

   D   an elephant

3 Give evidence from the poem to support your answers to questions 1 and 2.

_____

_____

_____

_____

_____

For question 4, choose the answer in which *both* phrases fit the blanks in the sentence.

4 In contrasting the two poems, it is accurate to say that "I Like to See it Lap the Miles" ____, while "The Runaway Engine" ____.

   A   expresses feelings…tells a story

   B   uses rhyme…does not use rhyme

   C   has a serious theme…has a humorous theme

   D   mostly uses plain language…mostly uses figurative language

5 How does the speaker in "I Like to See It Lap the Miles" feel about trains? Explain your answer using evidence from the poem.

_____

_____

_____

_____

6 Write a summary of "The Runaway Engine." In your summary, show how the structure of the poem develops stanza by stanza.

_____

_____

_____

_____

7 What is the theme of "The Runaway Engine"? How is it revealed in the challenges the engine faces and how it meets them?

_____

_____

_____

_____

Passage 1:

Farmers' Market

by Melinda Torvik

It's 10 a.m., and the Fremont Sunday Market is hopping. Farmers have finished unloading pickup trucks and are setting up their stalls. Customers are circulating through the market. A girl of about ten stands with her father behind a table. It is carpeted with cardboard baskets brimming with fresh raspberries. A brawny man in a railroad cap hoists watermelons from the bed of his truck. He tosses them one by one to a young man in a baseball cap. The young man fields them all without an error. He is building a pyramid of succulent-looking fruit. Beside him, a young woman takes flowers she has grown and fashions them into bouquets. Another woman sells frozen yogurt from an ice-cream truck. The milk she used to make it came from her own cows.

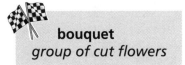

succulent
fruit or plant that is full of juice

The Fremont Sunday Market is in Seattle, Washington. You can see the city's landmark Space Needle beyond a high-arching bridge across a lake. But farmers' markets like it are proliferating across the United States. Growers outside the city bring in their produce and sell it directly to customers. Many city people see it as an appealing change from the supermarket.

"Where else can you find food this fresh?" says David Zhong. He's a regular customer at the market. Today, he's buying greens for what looks to be a world-class salad. "Most of this stuff was picked today or yesterday. You can't get fresher than that. And you want value? You buy food in the supermarket, it's been sold three or four times before it gets to you. Each time adds a little to the price. So does getting it from the farm to the city, from the wholesaler to the store. Here I know the growers personally. It's just a better way to buy food."

bouquet
group of cut flowers

A casual survey of three neighborhood stores confirms David's remark about value. As for freshness, judging by the melon slices Coral Dane is handing out as samples, the supermarkets just don't measure up.

Coral has been bringing her goods to Fremont for seven years. Her farm is near Monroe, a town about an hour's drive away. "It's too small to call a farm," Coral laughs. "It's more like a big backyard." Today, Coral is selling melons, cucumbers, lettuce, and green beans from her backyard. Later in the summer she'll have peppers, tomatoes, apples, and walnuts.

Coral has an acre planted in clover. "That's for the bees," she says, offering me a dab of honey on a piece of bread. Coral keeps eight hives on her land. The jars of honey on display at her stand range from a lemony yellow in color to a reddish brown. "Come back next month," she tells a customer. "Right now with the wild blackberries in bloom, there's a nectar run on."

The customer nods, waves, and walks away, three jars of honey in his bag. Then his attention is drawn by another stand, laden with fresh cherries. I spot him again a few minutes later. He and his small son are listening to a pair of musicians on flute and guitar. They're dipping into a bulging sack of cherries, chewing away absently as if snacking on popcorn at the movies.

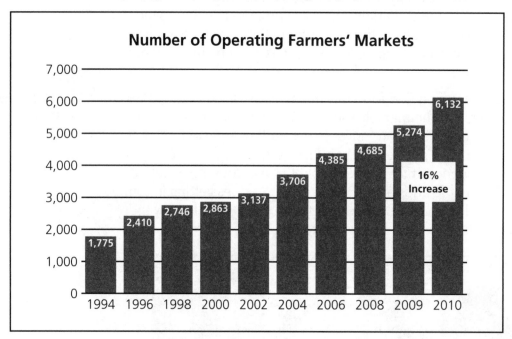

Number of Operating Farmers' Markets

Year	Number
1994	1,775
1996	2,410
1998	2,746
2000	2,863
2002	3,137
2004	3,706
2006	4,385
2008	4,685
2009	5,274
2010	6,132

16% Increase

Oldest Family Farm for Sale

New Hampshire Family Selling Their Land After 378 Years

by Peter Binford

The Tuttle family is selling their farm. Will Tuttle and his sisters Lucy and Becky are feeling their age and no longer have the energy to work the 134-acre spread near Dover, New Hampshire. They do not wish to pass along their way of life, not to mention a mountain of debt, to their children. In July 2010, the farm was advertised for sale.

Family farms have long been in decline in the United States. Every decade sees more of them bought up by large "agribusiness" farms or sold for development as housing and shopping malls. What makes this sale special is that the Tuttle farm has been owned by 11 generations of the Tuttle family. By some accounts, it's the oldest continually operating family farm in the United States—378 years old.

It all started with John Tuttle, who came to the colonies from England in 1632 with a grant from King Charles I to start a farm. After being shipwrecked off the Maine coast, he arrived at his 20 acres to find them covered with pine trees. He cut them down and planted his crops between the stumps. For the next 250 years, the Tuttles were subsistence farmers. They lived on what they grew. Then William Tuttle, the current owners' grandfather, increased the size of the farm to 200 acres. This allowed the family to produce more than they needed and sell it in nearby towns. William's son, Hugh Tuttle, adopted modern scientific farming methods and became known in his state for his work in soil and water conservation.

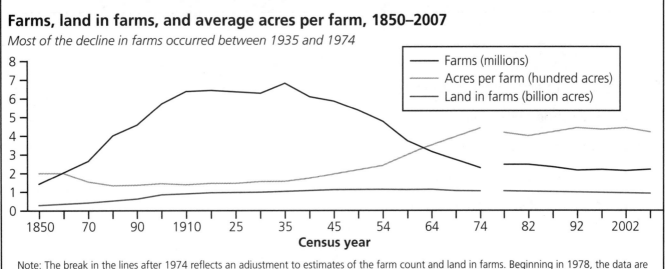

Farms, land in farms, and average acres per farm, 1850–2007

Most of the decline in farms occurred between 1935 and 1974

Legend:
— Farms (millions)
— Acres per farm (hundred acres)
— Land in farms (billion acres)

Census year: 1850, 70, 90, 1910, 25, 35, 45, 54, 64, 74, 82, 92, 2002

Note: The break in the lines after 1974 reflects an adjustment to estimates of the farm count and land in farms. Beginning in 1978, the data are adjusted to compensate for undercoverage by the Census of Agriculture. Source: USDA, Economic Research Service, compiled from Census of Agriculture data.

Hugh Tuttle died in 2002. His grown children kept the farm going for awhile by selling directly to customers. They made and sold cheeses, baked goods, nursery products, and other items from a stand on their property. However, many people find it more convenient to shop at supermarkets. The growth in popularity of farmers' markets also cut into the Tuttles' business. Even a small state like New Hampshire has more than 80 of them. More and more people are growing and preserving their own vegetables, even in cities.

Because of the conservation work done by Hugh Tuttle, the land cannot legally be sold for development. It will remain a farm. The Tuttles hope to find a buyer who loves the land the way they do. But for the first time in 378 years, it will not be owned by the Tuttle family.

8 In passage 1, the word <u>proliferating</u> means _____.

   A moving rapidly

   B causing problems

   C increasing in number

   D going out of business

9 In passage 1, what does Coral Dane mean by the idiom <u>nectar run</u>?

_____

_____

_____

_____

_____

10 The term <u>subsistence farmers</u> in passage 2 means farmers who _____.

   A own large areas of land

   B consume what they grow

   C sell their goods in markets

   D experiment with new kinds of crops

11 <u>Conservation</u> in passage 2 means ____.

   A not conserving

   B able to conserve

   C conserving again

   D the act of conserving

12 How does the graph following passage 1 help you answer question 8?

_____

_____

_____

_____

_____

13 Based on information in *both* passages, which of these is the *best* definition of a farmers' market?

   A a fruit and vegetable market in a big city

   B a market that is cheaper than a supermarket

   C a market that farmers set up on their own land

   D a market where growers sell directly to customers

14 Which of these *best* expresses the main idea of passage 2?

   A It's hard for a small family farm to stay in business nowadays.

   B After 378 years, the Tuttle family is selling their New Hampshire Farm.

   C Farmers' markets and supermarkets have forced the sale of the Tuttle family farm.

   D The Tuttle farm in New Hampshire may be the oldest family-owned farm in the United States.

15 Based on information in passage 2, what are three reasons the Tuttles are selling their farm?

_____

_____

_____

_____

_____

16 Both authors write about small farmers and how they market their goods. Compare and contrast the points of view of the two authors on this topic.

_____

_____

_____

_____

_____

17 How do the ways the two authors structure their articles show the differences in their points of view?

_____

_____

_____

_____

_____

18 Which of these statements about farmers' markets in passage 1 is an opinion?

   A Each time food is sold adds a little to the price.

   B Farmers' markets are a better way to buy food.

   C Food sold at supermarkets has been sold several times.

   D Growers at farmers' markets sell directly to the customers.

19 In passage 1, what evidence supports David Zhong's statement that food at the farmers' market is of better value and freshness than supermarket food?

_____

_____

_____

_____

20 Peter Binford states that "family farms have long been in decline in the United States." Does the graph included with his article support this statement? Explain why, or why not.

_____

_____

_____

_____

21 Which of these conclusions can you draw using information in *both* passages?

   A There are fewer farms in the United States now than there were 50 years ago.

   B More American food consumers these days are buying directly from growers.

   C The spread of farmers' markets may be able to save small farms like the Tuttles'.

   D Farms like the Tuttles' will probably be gone from the United States by the year 2060.

from **The Pirates of Korab-D**

by Richard Just

Colonel Wolf's office was as dull as I remembered, and every bit as menacing. Everything was gray and as hard as a ship's hull—the furniture, the computers, the lighting, the armed guards at the door, Wolf's hair. The only color came from space, the absurd candy stripes of the planet that filled half the curving window and glowed pale orange in the light of the distant sun.

Wolf grinned at me from behind his desk. "It's good to see you under restraints, Rain Holbrooke," he said. "Shu Raki, *gebora xaxati,*" he added in bad Jaarnese.

"Nice to see you too, Colonel," I said brightly. Raki's response was a growl.

The colonel gestured to a guard. "You can take those force rings off them; they aren't going anywhere," he said. The nastier-looking of the two goons thumbed a key on his belt console. The energy bands binding my arms and feet vanished with a soft zip. "Sit down," Wolf said.

"Thank you, but I'd rather stand." Raki remained silent, his Jaarnese eyes glowing watchfully at Wolf and his guards.

"As you wish, Rain," Wolf said. "You don't mind if I call you Rain, do you? 'Trader Holbrooke' would sound like I believe your legend, which I don't. I know you too well."

"I know you too, Colonel—you don't mind if I call you Colonel? 'Wolf' would sound like a comment on your personality, and I'd rather keep this strictly business."

"Very well, let's do that." He gave a voice command. The transparent glass of the space-station window became a curving view screen showing a three-dimensional map of the Fourteen Worlds. "You've no doubt heard about the space pirates that have been operating in sector Korab-D." The sector was highlighted on the screen. "With no offense meant to your navigator here, they're mostly Jaarnese and said to be led by a Jaarnese renegade named…uh…"

"Sarrakhin," Raki said. He bowed. "It's not his real name. Means 'warrior of the gods' in our ancient language."

"Sarrakhin," the colonel repeated. He was one of the few humans who could look at Raki eye-to-eye without appearing nervous. "Until now, the pirates have preyed mostly on independent traders like yourselves—human, alien, it's all the same to them. They steal the ships and their cargo, and the

Practice Test

crew are never heard from again—except for those who elect to join them, of which I understand there are a few.

"A week ago, Earth-standard, they captured a UEF cruiser with a crew of 109. That gives them serious firepower, not to mention 109 hostages. Sarrakhin is demanding safe passage to a planet beyond the sectors of the galaxy governed by the Fourteen Worlds. He wants you to be our negotiator with him—undoubtedly because he knows you fly with a Jaarnese."

"Undoubtedly," I said, with a glance at Raki. "Tell me, Colonel, what's in it for me if I agree?"

"A pardon for your crimes, including aiding the rebellion on Gambir's World."

I laughed in his face. "That was nine years ago. Nobody cares about that anymore. Not even you; tell the truth."

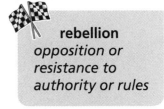

rebellion
opposition or resistance to authority or rules

"Sarrakhin won't negotiate in good faith," Raki spoke suddenly. "He'll end up with your planet, your cruiser, and 109 slaves. He imagines himself the last of the Holy Warriors of the conquering phase of our civilization. He spits on the Peace of Llangron and any other agreements my people have made with other races. That's why he was banished more than 300 of your people years ago."

Colonel Wolf leaned across his desk and said, "You seem to know a great deal about him, Shu Raki."

"I ought to," Raki said. "His real name is Shu Daarkan. He's…you would call him my first cousin."

from **Strange Music**

by Susan Harris

On Gabriela's World where the time winds blow, the past can be present and the future past. Few humans land there, and they do not stay long for fear of being displaced in time. Those who do may be treated to a sky that ranges blue to green to yellow under its two suns. They who are very lucky, or unlucky as it may be, have heard the Music.

Some say that the Music is the language of a long-vanished alien people. Others say that the Music is the thoughts and dreams of those who hear it. Some even say that Gabriela's World was spun from music and is made of music. One guess is as good as another, for everyone who hears the Music hears something different. An orchestra of strange and wonderful instruments. A lively band playing the happiest dance music that could ever be. A single flute playing a melody of surpassing beauty.

During a time of trouble on the worlds of humankind, a young man called Shaeto came to Gabriela's World.

He was 19 years old, give or take a thousand. He was neither short nor tall, neither large nor slender. Those who heard him play said that he had the warmest brown eyes they had ever seen, but they may have been responding to his music. He was a master of the Ugav and the Zil harp, and had studied such ancient Earth instruments as the guitar and violin. There are those who say his music plucked bouquets of flowers from their hearts. There are those who say his music could heal the sick and bring the dead to life. But there are those who will say anything.

Shaeto worked passage on a freighter bound for the Altair system. He jumped ship when it made a provisioning stop at the observation post near Gabriela's World. There he asked for shuttle transport to the planet's surface.

"Joyrider," the stationmaster sneered with a glance at Shaeto's instrument case. "Someone will take you down there for an hour, no longer."

"That's assuming you want a ride back," another staffer said with a laugh.

"I was planning to stay for a while," Shaeto said quietly.

"Don't you fear the time winds?" someone asked him.

"Not especially."

22 What is similar and what is different about these two stories? Use words like *character, theme,* and *genre* in answering this question.

_____

_____

_____

_____

_____

23 In "The Pirates of Korab-D," what is the challenge Rain and Raki will face?

_____

_____

_____

_____

_____

24 Raki's people are called the ____.

  A Korab

  B Gambir

  C Jaarnese

  D Sarrakhin

25 The first paragraph of "The Pirates of Korab-D" *mainly* establishes the ____.

  A plot

  B setting

  C character of Colonel Wolf

  D character of Rain Holbrooke

26 In "Strange Music," which of these is the topic sentence of the first paragraph?

  A On Gabriela's World where the time winds blow, the past can be present and the future past.

  B Few humans land there, and they do not stay long for fear of being displaced in time.

  C Those who do may be treated to a sky that ranges blue to green to yellow under its two suns.

  D They who are very lucky, or unlucky as it may be, have heard the Music.

27 Compare and contrast the points of view of the two stories. How do their points of view affect the way events are described?

_____

_____

_____

_____

_____

28 In "Strange Music," what do the idioms <u>worked passage</u> and <u>jumped ship</u> mean?

_____

_____

_____

_____

_____

29 What can you conclude about the characters of Rain, Raki, and Wolf from the way they interact with one another?

_____

_____

_____

_____

_____

30 Choose either of the pictures that illustrate these stories. How does the illustration help you to understand or appreciate the story?

_____

_____

_____

_____

_____

GLOSSARY

A

Abolitionist — before the Civil War, a person who sought an immediate end to slavery

Air — a song

Ajar — slightly open

Allegedly — according to what has been said

Alliteration — repeating the same consonant sounds

Amethyst — purple; a purple gemstone

Amphitheater — a round gathering space with seats rising from the center to create different levels

Antonyms — words with an opposite meaning

B

Ballad — narrative poem originally written to be sung

Ballistics — a scientific test used by police to determine from which gun a shot was fired

Bobolinks — a type of bird

Bouquet — group of cut flowers

C

Condense — to make denser or more compact

Couplet — two lines that rhyme in a poem

Courageous — brave

Climax — the high point of the story

D

Dame — lady, woman of noble birth

Debris — pieces of an object that has been broken down or destroyed

Definitions — words that tell what another word means

Democracy — rule by the people

Descriptions	words that tell you more about another word
Discipline	trained condition of order and obedience
Docile	gentle
Dominie	church minister or teacher

E

| **Enforcing** | causing to be followed |

F

Faience	type of pottery made of clay mixed with tin
Famine	severe food shortage
Featured	gave an important place to
Flashback	events that happened at an earlier time
Foreshadowing	suggestion that some event is to occur in the future
Free verse	poem that does not rhyme or have a rhythm
Fret	to worry

G

| **Genre** | type of literature |

H

Haiku	Japanese 17-syllable poem usually written in three lines
Hieroglyphics	form of writing that uses pictures to represent ideas and sounds
Homographs	words that are spelled the same but that have different meanings
Hyperbole	exaggerated statement for effect

I

| **Idioms** | phrase that means something other than the literal meaning |

L

| **Limerick** | humorous rhyming five-line poem |
| **Lyric Poem** | expresses the poet's feelings |

212

Glossary

M — **Martial Arts** sports based on skills once used in military combat

Melancholy feeling of depression

Metaphor type of figurative language that compares two unlike things but does not use *like* or *as*

Missionary a person sent to do work on behalf of a religion

N — **Narrative Poem** a poem that tells a story

O — **Oath** a promise

Omnipotent all-powerful

Onomatopoeia words that sound like what they are describing

Oppression the unjust act of being kept down by a higher authority

P — **Palatable** food that is agreeable enough to be eaten

Personification giving human characteristics to a concept or inanimate object

Piety religious feeling, or regard for one's parents

Pioneer settler in unexplored or unclaimed territory

Point of view who is telling the story

   first-person the main character is telling the story; uses first person pronouns *I* and *we*

   third-person limited omniscient narrator is limited to knowledge limited of the thoughts and feelings of only one of the characters; uses third-person pronouns *he, she,* and *they*

   third-person omniscient outside narrator is all-knowing and can reveal the thoughts and feelings of more than one of the characters; uses third-person pronouns *he, she,* and *they*

Portable an object that is easily moved or carried

Portal an entrance or gateway

Prefix part of a word added to beginning of another word that changes the meaning of the word

Prodigious huge

Prolific an abundance of something

Glossary 213

R   **Rebellion**   opposition or resistance to authority or rules

Reel   a country dance

Rhyme   repeated sounds at the ends of words

Rhythm   pattern of stressed and unstressed beat in a line of poetry

S   **Salmonella**   a type of bacteria that causes food poisoning

Scrimmage   struggle, or playing a sport for practice

Simile   type of figurative language that compares two unlike things using *as* or *like*

Sonnet   a 14-line poem that follows a specific rhyme scheme

Sparse   thinly scattered

Spires   tall, slender objects that taper to a point, like a church steeple

Squirmed   to show embarrassment; twist like a worm

Stanza   a group of lines within a poem, similar to a chapter within a book

Sterilized   made free from living germs

Steward   someone who manages another's property or business dealings

Stile   step or set of steps for climbing over a wall or fence

Succulent   fruit or plant that is full of juice

Suffix   part of a word added to the end of another word that changes the meaning of the word

Supercilious   proud and scornful

Synonyms   words that have a similar meaning

T   **Tepid**   neither hot nor cold

Transition   act of changing from one place, form, or activity to another

U   **Underground Railroad**   a secret network of people who helped slaves escape to freedom

Vandalism	destroying or damaging property
Vanity	too much pride in one's own self
Visage	face